Chicano Satire

Mexican American Monographs, No. 14
Sponsored by the Center for Mexican American Studies
The University of Texas at Austin

CHICANO SATIRE
A Study in Literary Culture

by Guillermo E. Hernández

 University of Texas Press, Austin

First Edition, 1991

Requests for permission to reproduce material from this work
should be sent to Permissions, University of Texas Press, Box
7819, Austin, Texas 78713-7819.

⊗ The paper used in this publication meets the minimum
requirements of American National Standard for Information
Sciences—Permanence of Paper for Printed Library Materials,
ANSI Z39.48-1984.

Library of Congress Cataloging-in-Publication Data

Hernández, Guillermo, 1940–
  Chicano satire : a study in literary culture / by Guillermo E.
Hernández. — 1st ed.
      p.   cm. — (Mexican American monographs ; no. 14)
  Includes bibliographical references and index.
  ISBN 0-292-71123-9 (alk. paper)
  1. American literature—Mexican American authors—History
and criticism.   2. Satire, American—Mexican American au-
thors—History and criticism.   3. Mexican Americans—In-
tellectual life.   4. Mexican Americans in literature.
I. Title.   II. Series.
PS153.M4H47   1991
817'.540986872—dc20   90-43757
                                                  CIP

Para:
Arturo
Luciano
Guillermo
Gabriel

Contents

Preface

Writing on Chicano literature involves entering a new field of inquiry, one that has grown largely at the margins of the American literary mainstream and is generally ignored in the Spanish-speaking world. It is an area that has been accorded the benign neglect of major publishing houses and academic institutions albeit the numerous creative and critical works by Chicano writers and scholars that have appeared in diverse publications during the last twenty years. As a consequence, readers of Chicano literature have depended on specialized presses publishing new titles, and texts that not long ago received praise for their artistic merit are now out of print. Courses in Chicano literature, as other curricula in the emerging field of Chicano studies, when tolerated, are often treated as remnants of past political compromises and too frequently are perceived as tenuous academic endeavors. This situation has had a number of implications in the study of Chicano literature. On the one hand, it has allowed a small and committed group of writers and scholars the autonomy to work and dialogue on diverse issues related to Chicano literature. On the other hand, it has kept at arm's length a wide range of comparative approaches and views that undoubtedly would have enriched the field.

It is unfortunate, moreover, that many studies that profess to be on Chicanos have contributed little to our knowledge of Chicano life and culture, while fundamental questions in the area remain to be addressed. At one extreme are research efforts whose major purpose, being ancillary to Chicano studies, could have been as easily satisfied in the study of any other ethnic or social grouping in the United States. At the other extreme are studies designed principally to help validate personal experience or opinion. Additionally, there is an urgent need in Chicano scholarship for the retrieval and preservation of cultural history before important documentation is lost or falls into oblivion. One such list would include oral histories, newspapers, theatrical scripts, memories, unknown published and unpublished manuscripts, recordings, songs, photographs, drawings, paintings, letters, and the like. The relative scarcity of such materials has encouraged Chicano literary researchers to circumscribe their studies to the examination of contemporary texts. This attention to recent literary works is necessary and most valuable, but when the research is conducted ahistorically or without knowledge—or acknowledgment—of the complex contexts involved, the result can only be fragmentary and, when thus disconnected from the literature or the culture of the people that gave it life, bereft of either meaning or significance.

Given these limitations, and wishing to escape some of their pitfalls, I have opted to provide an intertextual approach to the examination of Chicano literary works—from various regions, perspectives, and genres—by placing them within a larger cultural framework. I emphasize how historical circumstances in Chicano communities produce cultural paradigms that appear in literary texts as evaluative frameworks to be applied in the analysis of Chicano conduct. I argue that, given the predominant influences that Anglo-American and Mexican cultural values exert on Chicano life, the critical interpretation of Chicano texts must be particularly sensitive to in-group perspectives. My focus is on an important aspect in Chicano discourse: the use of humor and invective in the creation of a literary culture. The introduction gives the reader an overview of satire—my generic and theoretical focal point—as well as some salient characteristics in Chicano satirical culture, especially its ties to Spanish and Mexican norms. I lament the many information gaps in the study and look forward to the day when important collections of documents allow for more precise approaches to Chicano culture.

In the chapters that follow the introduction, I examine the text of three important contemporary Chicano authors: Luis Valdez, José Montoya, and Rolando Hinojosa. The generic conventions that the writers employ differ: Valdez is a dramatist; Montoya, a poet; and Hinojosa, a novelist. Their works also reflect their different personalities, upbringings, and regional backgrounds: the first is a Californian; the second, a New Mexican transplanted to California; and the third, a Texan. In spite of these differences, the three authors share a number of comparable experiences: they grew up in bilingual rural communities and personally underwent processes of urban acculturation. In addition, they are highly educated (Valdez and Montoya have master's degrees; Hinojosa received a doctorate) and are prominent in their professions. The three showed unequivocal signs of artistic vocation before the 1960s and 1970s, yet it was during this period that their talents were realized and publicly recognized. Their creative efforts, although pursued independently of each other, have offered new perspectives on the Chicano experience, and their respective reformulations of Chicano culture may be said to be a most significant contribution of their satires.

This book is neither a comparative examination nor an exhaustive study of the works of Luis Valdez, José Montoya, and Rolando Hinojosa. Rather, it is a preliminary inquiry into an important phenomenon in cultural studies: the characteristics and evolution of Chicano satire, a genre especially suited for the study of conflict. Yet, I do not propose to examine here solely a discordant minority expression; I argue, instead, that Chicano satirical discourse must be perceived as part of the contemporary discussion on the nature and significance of canonical and noncanonical texts. In this larger sense (other than at an in-group, immediate level) Chicano satire reveals its cogency: it must be recognized as part of a literary culture embedded in a dialogical discourse that includes a wide range of voices—European and non-European; Anglo- and Latin American; majority and minority; normative and deviant, ancient and new.

I wish to express my gratitude to many of the individuals and institutions who helped me complete this book. I am indebted to the Committee on Research at the University of California, Los Angeles, which has supported my research. The Department of Spanish and Portuguese at UCLA gave me time and support in the writing of the manuscript. I owe much to my students, graduate and undergraduate, Chicanos and non-Chicanos, whose questions, discussions, and patience, throughout the years, encouraged me to conceptualize many of the ideas in this book. In the preparation of the manuscript, I received the kind help of Candelyn Candelaria and Eleuteria Hernández. Theresa May, Barbara Spielman, and Barbara Cummings from the University of Texas Press have been most kind and patient editors.

I also wish to attest the valuable assistance of numerous friends and colleagues who read part or all of the manuscript as it progressed. I want to thank Shirley L. Arora, Rubén Benítez, Carroll B. Johnson, José Miguel Oviedo, Ray Rocco, and Gerardo Luzuriaga. I am especially grateful to Raymund Paredes, Juan Velasco, and José Monleón for their many valuable suggestions and commentaries. The authors, Luis Valdez, José Montoya, and Rolando Hinojosa, whose works I analyze, gave generously of their time, confidence, and assistance and allowed me to conduct taped interviews. I only hope this study conveys the great admiration I feel for their talent. I also wish to acknowledge some satirist friends who over the years have informally taught me the art of verbal satire: Charley Trujillo, Ramón Lerma, Arnoldo Vásquez, Alvaro Sánchez, and Aurora Zepeda.

My thanks also to Yolanda, who, beyond tolerable limits, never fails to give me her patience, support, and suggestions on my thinking, research, and writing and who has endured the evolution of this book from isolated ideas into a finished manuscript.

Chicano Satire

1. Satire: An Introduction

Satire is frequently associated with ancient Roman writers. For many scholars the works of Lucilius, Horace, Juvenal, Persius, and Seneca, among others, stand as the initiators and models of the genre. The term *satire* is also identified with a number of English authors of the seventeenth and eighteenth centuries, such as Dryden, Pope, Swift, and Defoe. Thus, while research on the Roman and English art of satire has grown considerably, especially during the last fifty years, it is a genre rarely considered when studying other traditions or periods. Yet, the term *satire* has generally had two distinct connotations: it is employed in a restricted sense to discuss specific texts—usually referring to the Roman and English models—or else it is broadly applied to a wide range of expressions.[1] Because this inconsistent practice involves a variety of generic discourses, defining satire and distinguishing it from other rhetorical conventions has remained an elusive if not a debatable subject.[2]

In spite of the many difficulties posed by the study of satire—particularly its resistance to fit into a neat definition—the attempts to identify it have enriched our knowledge of the genre.[3] Most of us can agree, for example, with Samuel Johnson's assessment of satire as an attack against someone or something considered to merit opposition. Likewise, few can object to the observation that the target of satiric attack is likely to be a fictional entity whose historical reality may or may not be apparent.[4] It is also generally accepted that satire exists along a continuum that extends from one extreme of invective to another of the comic or, as Northrop Frye suggests, that satire maintains an equilibrium between tragedy and comedy. Indeed, as Robert C. Elliott has pointed out, there exists great variability within the corpus of satire:

> No strict definition can encompass the complexity of a word that signifies, on one hand, a kind of literature—as when one speaks of the satires of the Roman poet Horace or calls the American novelist Nathan[ael]

West's *A Cool Million* a satire—and, on the other, a mocking spirit or tone that manifests itself in many literary genres but can also enter into almost any kind of human communication. Wherever wit is employed to expose something foolish or vicious to criticism, there satire exists, whether it be in song or sermon, in painting or political debate, on television or in the movies. In this sense satire is everywhere. ("Satire" 182)

In the Western tradition, satire is associated with a number of stereotyped figures who are customarily subjected to hostility, humor, or else indifference. These negative figures may ultimately be traced to marginal groups or individuals who are frequently subjected to censure or abuse. Characteristics attributed to the marginal naturally are considered a normative deviation and stand in opposition to the ideal principles and behavior upheld by a dominant group. Thus, stigmatized members of a social group may be subjected to the antagonism or even the hatred of majorities who feel threatened, as occurred in Germany to the Jews, the Gypsies, and the handicapped during World War II. But a more common response toward the marginal, when not perceived as an immediate threat to the established notions of power and prestige, is censure, ridicule, or indifference. Such tensions create conditions that enable satire to prosper. Satire has, therefore, a direct relationship to social history. It is a genre that—along with others to which it is closely allied: comedy, humor, jest, parody, wit, irony, and so forth—includes a variety of rhetorical devices designed to represent the marginal.

In the ridicule made of foreigners and their alien traits such as language, customs, and values, there lies an implicit reaffirmation of the linguistic, social, and ethical standards of a dominant group. This quality of marginality, however, is not confined to individuals recognized as distinctively extraneous to a group. The whore and the cuckold, for example, are figures that contrast markedly with the dignified stance of the faithful couple—a model embodying the ideals of love and marriage in a given social order. A parallel function underlies such figures as the madman, the sinner, the fool, the delinquent, the miser, the coward, and the cripple, negative characters who have positive counterparts in the portrayal of the ruler, the saint, the sage, the citizen, the patron, the hero, and the athlete. The Hegemonic Spectrum is a fragmentary, conceptual version of those values and figures that represent the norm and its deviations. It is a framework that explains the mutual dependency that exists between normative and deviant qualities.

On the extreme left of the Hegemonic Spectrum is a list of negative values that represent basic threats to human existence. These general abstractions convey the idea of exclusion, dispossession, and

Hegemonic Spectrum

Negative			Positive	
Nonbeing (General Abstraction)	Marginal (Fictional Figure)		Normative (Fictional Figure)	Being (General Abstraction)
Chaos	Madman	H	Ruler	Order
Evil	Sinner	i	Saint	Good
Ignorance	Fool	s	Sage	Knowledge
Violence	Delinquent	t	Citizen	Peace
Destitution	Miser	o	Patron	Wealth
Fear	Coward	r	Hero	Courage
Infirmity	Cripple	i	Athlete	Health
		c		
	Prostitute	a	Beloved	
	Spinster	l	Bride	
Sexual disintegration	Widow		Wife	Sexual integration
	Lecher	A	Lover	
	Homosexual	x	Groom	
	Cuckold	i	Husband	
	Stepmother	s	Mother	
Alienation	The Other		The Subject	Harmony

death, hence generally are associated with alienation or nonbeing. On the extreme right are their opposites, depicting life-oriented principles of harmony or being.[5] These two extremes arise from the concrete experience of a people and represent the standards by which individuals and groups measure the meaning and significance of their lives.[6] Social groups recognize both of these categories metaphorically through fictional figures that personify the ideal (normative) and the negative (marginal), also identified as the subject and the other, and listed respectively as the second and third columns.[7] The historical axis—located as a middle column—depicts actual experience, serving as a mediation between harmony and alienation and their respective personifications as fictional figures.[8] Implicit in the ideal figures are their unfavorable counterparts and, conversely, the representation of the negative involves their positive contraries. That is, these fictional figures are in a dialectical relationship: one cannot exist or be mentioned without overtly or tacitly acknowledging the presence and influence of a logical opposite.

But it must be noted that these negative and positive figures are not depicted solely according to the basic outline suggested in the Hegemonic Spectrum. The *Characters* of Theophrastus, for instance, demonstrates how the personification of single values can only produce what E. M. Forster (67) has called "flat" or "two-dimensional people." Thus, the hero is likely to be portrayed as a courageous individual who also possesses strength, knowledge, and sexual integration and who might be represented as a ruler, an athlete, a sage, or a blending of these roles and their characteristics. The coward, for example, may show fear as well as reflect ignorance, destitution, infirmity, and sexual disintegration while adopting the personalities and traits of the madman, the sinner, and the delinquent. Therefore, even though each of these figures may be associated with a predominant attribute—positive or negative—its personification is likely to borrow from various other kindred qualities.[9]

These figures are intelligible only within particular cultural contexts, since their significance is evident only in relation to the specific conventions of a group.[10] This grounding in history explains the evolution of fictional figures. The marginal, for instance, may be identified at various times with the barbarian, the demonic, the mentally ill, or an exponent of a false philosophy, religion, or political belief. At various historical periods, the concept of wisdom has been depicted according to the principles established by art, science, or economics. Similarly, as Joseph Campbell (391) has demonstrated, the figure of the ideal man may appear as a hunter, a warrior, or a soldier. In contemporary times the hero is often depicted as a spy, a detective, or a space traveler, lonely figures that must pursue individual quests within inhospitable and threatening worlds.

The Hegemonic Spectrum, however, includes a few representative categories and figures that have become conventional in Western tradition. A comprehensive schema would require a discussion of all the possible values and figures that cultural groups have devised to stand for the norms and their corresponding deviant doubles. Indeed, religions, tribes, regional and ethnic groups, nations, professions, classes, fraternal organizations, and any other social groupings, formal and informal, that appeal to their members' solidarity will deploy figures that represent the norms in opposition to their marginal parallels. For present purposes, however, this paradigm may suffice as an illustration of the dialectical relationship that exists between the negative and the positive values of a group.

The Hegemonic Spectrum provides a conceptual framework that can help us understand some fundamental differences between satire and comedy—the way in which each genre offers a distinct treatment of the marginal—and the assumptions held by their authors and audiences. In comedy those who are marginal are subjected to ridicule or abuse, but this debasement serves principally to amuse by reinforcing established norms, given that comic figures, as inoffensive beings, do not challenge the values and symbols of the status quo. The satiric attack, in contrast, has a primary purpose to ridicule and invalidate the normative principles and interpretations upheld by victims who are portrayed with scorn. Consequently, the satirist frequently is perceived as a subversive whose art represents an opposing, incompatible, and overwhelming evaluative norm that challenges the legitimacy of cherished normative values and figures.[11] The history of literary culture includes many satirists who have been censured, punished, exiled, and even murdered for ridiculing the beliefs and attributes of powerful figures or groups.

The satiric attack, however, may be concealed through dissembling techniques, as modern students of satire have discovered. For instance, an author may adopt the persona of an unreliable narrator whose dramatic function is to discredit the voice of the first-person narrator. Yet another difference between the two genres is that comedy does not place in doubt the group's hegemony, while satire *does* cast such doubt. Indeed, satire's repertoire includes figures who are treated or perceived in marginal terms, but who represent a rival norm.[12] Since the abstract values shown in the Hegemonic Spectrum are intangibles in the sense that they serve as general conceptions common to all human existence (the notions of order, knowledge, wealth, chaos, ignorance, fear, destitution, and the like, only acquire meaning when rendered within the conventions of a particular cultural group), it follows then that historically the normative figures that evolve from emergent cultures will displace those that represent a declining or weaker hegemony.[13] Satire is also present when rival groups appeal to the loyalty of members who must decide upon the validity of opposing value systems.[14] The evolution of satire is thus a fine register of cultural change and a record of the ingenuity of groups to gain ascendancy over normative space.

The presence of this normative-deviant polarity may open possibilities in the analysis of the discourse of "the subject" as well as in the reexamination, or recovery, of discourses ("the other") that have been (are) customarily silenced, ignored, or discredited—for example, those of alternative gender, ethnic, racial, or class persuasions. From this polar opposition may be drawn a number of important implications

1. Human conduct is characterized by a continuous attempt to acquire, preserve, or deny normative privilege.
2. The *subject* and the *other* are concepts that fundamentally discriminate what is personal, familiar, or understandable from what is alien, strange, or unknown.
3. The *other* is largely an imaginary creation of the *subject* to represent an antithetical (generally negative) image of ideal values and practices.
4. The *subject* cannot exist without the *other* and vice versa.
5. The *subject* creates elaborate principles, procedures, and systems—that is, ideologies, laws, and institutions—that serve to justify and enforce the validity of norms and to discredit, oppose, or silence the deviations associated with the *other*.
6. Norms and deviations are abstractions that only acquire meaning when encoded within the distinctive cultural conventions of specific groups in particular historical circumstances.
7. Literary texts, conventions, and authors (also teachers, critics, and theoreticians) are instrumental in the affirmation or rejection of normative paradigms.

In the discussion that follows, I assume that Chicano cultural history is inscribed in the satiric discourse of Chicano literary texts.[15] This discourse, as we shall see, is an in-group response to the distinctive perspectives derived from historical experience. That is, since a significant period of Chicano history has existed within the confines of two intersecting and frequently conflictive cultural domains—the Mexican and the Anglo-American normative models—Chicano satirists have expressed diverse attitudes toward these conditions.[16]

The Varieties of the Chicano Experience

Cultural variation among Chicanos is of fundamental importance. The Spanish-speaking population who until the nineteenth century inhabited what is now the southwestern United States shared a great many similarities with other colonial groups throughout Spanish America. The role of this group in establishing the foundations of Chicano culture, however, has yet to be properly acknowledged.[17] The constant immigration to the United States from Mexico since the second half of the past century has provided another significant cultural current. This immigrant influence—consisting mostly of workers and their families from rural areas in central and northern Mexico—was particularly prominent during the Mexican Revolution (1910–1920) and the Bracero Program (1942–1947). Beginning during World War I, but especially after World War II, a cultural variant emerged whose objectives included active participation in Anglo-American sociocultural life. Identified as Mexican American, this group entered the public sphere along with other ethnic groups from various national origins and with similarly constructed names: that is, Irish Americans, Italian Americans, and so forth. While still maintaining a strong Mexican cultural identity, Mexican Americans gained entry into many areas of American economic, political, and cultural life that until 1940 had rarely included Spanish-surnamed Americans.

In the 1960s there arose among the people of Mexican descent in the United States a heightened sense of their historical existence.[18] This experience, until then absorbed largely within a familial or interfamilial focus, during this decade began to be formulated as a discourse that transcended the limits of the immediate community and soon became unified under the in-group term Chicano. During this period, and as an artistic consequence of this new perspective, Chicano creative writers helped to forge a vital literary movement, and a new generation of authors emerged who felt encouraged to express themes and viewpoints that until then were considered unworthy of artistic representation.[19] The climate in which this name was adopted has provided it with its political connotations.[20] Finally, a more recent cultural perspective—often associated with the term *Hispanic*—has been used to include the post-1970s emerging urban middle-class professionals who, as had some of their Mexican American predecessors, have sought total integration into diverse areas of the American cultural mainstream (Treviño 71).

Although these various Chicano cultural groupings have appeared at distinct historical periods, frequent overlappings occur. It is thus plausible, for example, for a family to include members with contrasting cultural features: that is, a woman imbued with a colonial cultural perspective married to a Mexican immigrant whose children identify themselves, their experiences, or aspirations as either Mexican, Mexican American, Chicano, or Hispanic. Indeed, all these cultural or historical currents discussed ought not to be considered rigidly nor in isolation from each other. Many other cultural complexities could be found. In the communities of Mexican origin in the Midwest, for example, an immigrant population predominates, whereas in areas along the Mexican border an active biculturalism erases the sharp distinctions among the various cultural currents. Additional or alternative distinctions could certainly be drawn based on gender, class, age, racial makeup, regional origin, economics, or a combination of these as well as other characteristics. In actual practice a people's culture is best perceived as an uneven continuum with detours, gaps, and, as is generally observed when discussing cultural taxonomy, with frequent blending, exceptions, and incidence of ambivalence.

A cursory examination of Chicano texts reveals how cultural diversity is intimately linked to contrasting historical perspectives and the emergence of literary themes. For example, in a novel published in San Francisco in 1885 (*The Squatter and the Don*, written by María Amparo Ruiz Burton under the pseudonym C. Loyal), the presence of an external, alien, Anglo world overpowering the familiarity and comfort of Mexican culture is central. This response is portrayed by a member of the Spanish-speaking elite who lost their privileged status after the United States occupied the Californian territories during the nineteenth century. Ruiz Burton's work is important insofar as it voices some significant historical events surrounding the lives of the native inhabitants known as Californios.

In contrast to Ruiz Burton's criticism stands Leo Carrillo's *The California I Love* (1961), a nostalgic reconstruction of the author's family past when caballeros and señoritas presumably led a genteel life, singing and dancing while upholding admirable ancestral virtues. Carrillo's pride is founded on his descent from Californian founding families, a social and cultural legacy that enhances his life and provides him with dignity in an Anglo-American world. Thus, Carrillo's perspective is a variant Mexican American testimony of the colonial and postcolonial experience, filtered through family memoirs. His autobiography illustrates the pride felt by a Spanish-speaking Californian whose lineage allegedly posits him in a superior social and cultural status. Both Ruiz Burton and Carrillo lament the loss of property and social standing and look with nostalgia toward the past.

A markedly different response is offered by Texan Chicanos who deeply resented the abuses Anglo-Texans perpetrated on their communities. Such feelings appear in ballads such as "El Corrido de Gregorio Cortez" (1901), studied by Américo Paredes in *"With His Pistol in His Hand."* The dilemma posed by Gregorio Cortez is essentially an ethical one and may be stated as follows: violence is totally justified whenever an individual acts to defend self and family in an interethnic conflict and under a system devoid of due process. To his contemporary Tejanos (Mexican Texans), the figure of Cortez soon became a symbol of their conflictive history during the previous fifty years. Because his figure embodied many deeply felt issues among Chicanos, his heroic exploits transcended an immediate audience, and his ballad continues to be sung today throughout the United States and northern Mexico.

Another literary example is provided by J. Humberto Robles in his play *Los desarraigados* (1962). In this drama an older Mexican immigrant couple who reside in the United States suffer exploitation and homesickness as they helplessly watch the self-defeat of their children, who grow up amid moral decadence. The protagonist in the play is a rebellious upper middle-class young woman from Mexico City who reconverts into a dutiful daughter and becomes fully appreciative of the superior cultural values of Mexican society, after observing the plight of her Mexican immigrant hosts in the United States. Her decision to return to Mexico solves her immediate personal conflict, but this denouement has larger significance, since it involves a comparison between the moral values of Mexico and those of the United States. The message of the play is that Chicano problems are self-inflicted and would cease to exist upon their return to Mexico, where there still is morality, family integrity, and the possibility of achieving a fulfilling life.

A contrasting perspective is provided by Richard Rodriguez in *Hunger of Memory* (1982). In this autobiographical account, Rodriguez asserts his Americanism by pointing out every possible social and cultural element that no longer identifies him as a Mexican. Drawing from his individual experience, Rodriguez portrays himself as a cultural martyr whose assimilation has led to alienation from his parents, his studies, and his cultural roots. This loss, however, is a necessary step for his evolution as a sophisticated urban intellectual. Rodriguez's basic tenet is that total Chicano assimilation into Anglo-American life represents the only viable alternative for the children of Mexican immigrants.

The texts of Robles and Rodriguez do not allow for the existence of a Chicano historical perspective that deviates from a strict notion of what is genuinely Mexican or American.[21] The implicit claim in both works is that Chicanos must adhere to "legitimate" cultural norms. Theirs are the views held in the cultural mainstream of Mexico and of the United States, where Chicanos have been portrayed as anomalies suffering alienation either from Mexican culture or else as the result of a deficient assimilation into Anglo-American cultural patterns. It is not surprising, therefore, that upon their publication, *Los desarraigados* and *Hunger* were respectively given the immediate and enthusiastic support of influential and sympathetic circles.[22]

Undoubtedly, both Mexican and Anglo-American influence have been important in the shaping of Chicano culture. In spite of their presence for several generations before the arrival of Anglo-Americans in the territories that are now the United States, prior to World War II the status of Chicanos remained as that of aliens or "Mexicans." Indeed, during this period Chicano cultural identity and community life remained relatively isolated and unknown to outsiders and was closely aligned to Mexico.[23] Yet, the demographic changes that have occurred since the first quarter of the twentieth century have brought many Chicanos into a wide range of Anglo-American sociocultural areas. One key factor in the interpretation of Chicano culture, therefore, lies in recognizing the various strategies that Chicanos have devised for over a hundred and fifty years in blending, adapting, reformulating, accepting or rejecting, one set of cultural values or the other.

The Anglo-American impact on this northernmost Mexican, or southernmost American, population during the nineteenth century is a revealing indicator of the role the United States has played toward its Spanish-speaking continental neighbors. From this perspective the cultural history of Chicanos is, in many important ways, a microcosm of the relationship between Latin America and the United States. The roots of Anglo-American antagonism toward Spaniards, Mexicans—and, by implication, other Latin Americans—has been the subject of an excellent study by Raymund Paredes, who summarizes his findings as follows: "When Americans began actually to encounter Mexicans in Texas, Santa Fe, and other Mexican territories after 1821, their initial responses were conditioned primarily by the traditions of hispanophobia and anti-Catholicism. . . . Other 19th-century responses to Mexicans reveal the same process: old images received new justifications and lived on. Some are with us still" ("The Origins" 158).[24]

But for Chicanos the disdain of Mexicans can also represent a conflictive issue. At a time (1913) when the Mexican Revolution caused alarm in the United States and American intervention seemed an imminent possibility, the New Mexican Elfego Baca ironically pointed out:

> Sobre todo al tiempo de que hubiera intervención los Hispano-Americanos en los Estados Unidos vendríamos a quedar más mal que a la presente estamos, porque en México no nos quieren por agringados y en los Estados Unidos tampoco porque llevamos el nombre Mexicano. . . . Este es el juego de la correa, si la ensarta pierde y si no también. (Cited in "Los Mexicanos")

> [So, if there is to be an invasion, we Hispano-Americans in the United States would be worse off than we are now because they do not want us in Mexico, since we have acculturated ("gringoized") to the Anglo,

and neither are we accepted in the United States because we are Mexicans. . . . This is like the game of the strap, you lose whether you put it in or not.]

Baca's attitude anticipates by many decades the critical perspective that surfaced among Chicano groups during the 1960s. He thus acknowledges the inadequate conditions of his people: "más mal que a la presente estamos" (worse than we are now), while calling for a united front to recognize their cultural distance from Mexico as well as differences with Anglo-Americans. This is a reference to the complex history of Chicanos and to the variety of perspectives that inform their responses. His allusion to Mexico and the United States is also a recognition of a double cultural influence: the former provides an in-group perspective, while the latter represents an outside world that must be conquered at an individual level.[25] This intertwined evaluating process must precede any discussion in the history of Chicano discourse and requires observing the shift from a Mexican-oriented cultural base to an Anglo-American frame of reference.[26]

Chicano Comic and Satiric Figures

An early observer of Anglo-American influence on Mexican communities was the Mexican Lieutenant José María Sánchez, who during the years 1828 and 1829 served as a member of the Comisión de Límites en la Frontera con Texas (Commission to Oversee the Border Limits with Texas). In his diary of his travel to the United States—Mexican border region, Lieutenant Sánchez described a Mexican group who showed signs of cultural assimilation:

> The Mexicans that live here are very humble people, and perhaps their intentions are good, but because of their education and environment they are ignorant not only of the customs of our great cities, but even of the occurrences of our Revolution, excepting a few persons who have heard about them. Accustomed to the continued trade with the North Americans, they have adopted their customs and habits, and one may say truly that they are not Mexicans except by birth, for they even speak Spanish with marked incorrectness. (283)

Implicit in this commentary is a sense of alienation toward Chicanos that is still found today among many observers from Mexico. In thus excluding them as cultural peers, Lieutenant Sánchez fails to realize that an Anglo-American observer during this period would consider the group as Mexican. Indeed, the population at Nacogdoches described by Sánchez was subjected to continuous abuse during the same period, and ten years later, in 1838, according to Arnoldo De León, "many Mexicans were killed or expelled" from the region (*They Called Them Greasers* 78).

Sánchez' observation, however, does not yet carry the derogatory tone employed two decades later toward the Mexican women who befriended the North American soldiers who invaded Mexico during the war of 1848 and 1849. In his memoirs Antonio García Cubas recalls a popular song of the period, "La pasadita," where the behavior of these women is ridiculed:

> Ya las Margaritas
> hablan el Inglés
> les dicen: me quieres
> y responden: *yes.*
> *mi entende de monis*
> *mucho güeno está.* (443)

> ["Today Margaritas
> speak English
> they are told: Do you love me?
> and they say: *yes.*
> Me understand about *moneys*
> is much good."]

This song reveals several aspects that will eventually play a significant role in the figure of the *pocho*. The parody made of the peasant dialect, with an evident Indian influence: "mucho güeno está" (is much good) reflects the social position of these women, accused by García Cubas as being "meretrices de ínfima calidad" (the lowest type of prostitutes). In the song it is implied that only dishonorable Mexican women would establish relations with the invading enemy soldiers and, then, certainly guided by questionable values. This accusation is synthesized in linguistic terms through the mockery of their awkward imitation of English: "mi entende de monis" (me understand about *moneys*). The *pocho* often will be associated with this linguistic and cultural stigma, and his portrayal may also involve the representation of dishonesty in contrast to the virtues implicit in the observance of traditional Mexican norms.[27]

An important aspect of this song, and a customary feature in Mexican culture, is the parody of the dialects spoken by peasants and Indians. This is conventional in Western culture whereby the rustic is deemed inferior to the urban inhabitant, and characteristics of the fool are attributed to rural behavior.[28] There are many antecedents of this practice in literary history. Thus, in the fifteenth century, Juan de la Encina employed the Sayagüés dialect in order to achieve a humorous effect in his theatrical representations. Later, other Spanish authors of comedy and drama portrayed the rustic as a comic figure—first as a *villano*, or villager, and then as a courtly *gracioso*—whose linguistic lapses into dialectal forms or grammatical "mistakes" served to release dramatic tension. In the New World, too, colonial writers—including Fernán González de Eslava (1534–1601?), Mateo Rosas de Oquendo (1559?–?), Sor Juana Inés de la Cruz (1651–1695), and Eusebio Vela (1688–1737)—introduced the expressions of native dialects and dialectal Spanish in their portrayal of comic types.[29] This convention is also evident in the first Mexican novel, which appeared as a newspaper serial in 1816, *El periquillo sarniento*, where the picaresque protagonist, Perico, describes his encounter in jail with a naive rustic who seeks his help.

> —Pues ha de saber usted que me llamo *Cemeterio Coscojales*.
> —Eleuterio, dirá usted—Le respondí—, o Emeterio, porque *Cemeterio* no es nombre de santo.
> —Una cosa ansí me llamo . . . (Fernández de Lizardi 206)

> ["You should know that my name is *Cemeterio Coscojales*."
> "You mean Eleuterio," I answered him, "or Emeterio, because *Cemeterio* is not a saint's name."
> "Something like that is my name . . . "]

Here the comic note consists in suggesting that the rustic does not know his own name and, consequently, has a confused sense of identity. This foolishness leads him to mispronounce Cemeterio—a nonexisting name that resembles the word *cementerio* (cemetery)—instead of the probable Emeterio or Eleuterio, as would correspond within the tradition of naming children after the saints commemorated on their birthdays.

On another occasion Perico accidentally bumps into a peddler of pottery who berates him for destroying his merchandise:

> Un diablo se volvió luego que se sintió lastimado de mi mano, y entre mexicano y castellano me dijo:
> —*Tlacatecotl*, mal diablo, *Lacrón* jijo de un dimoño; ahora lo veremos quien es cada cual. (266)

> [He turned against me, like a devil, and feeling the hurt I had caused him, said, speaking half Castilian and half Mexican: "*Tlacatecotl*, devil, *thief* son of a *demon*; we'll now see who is who."]

In this scene the helpless rage of the humble seller who is incapable of expressing himself in Standard Spanish is depicted as ridiculous.[30] Thus, we see that in New Spain the prototype of the peninsular rustic underwent a metamorphosis, evolving into the figure of a peasant mestizo or an Indian.

A significant example of this attitude toward the Mexican rural classes was present during the latter part of the nineteenth century in the attack Guillermo Prieto directed against Juan Nepomuceno Almonte, pointing out the latter's Indian ancestry and the incongruity this represented to his role as promoter of a French intervention in Mexico:

> Amo quinequi, Juan Pamuceno,
> no te lo plantas el Majestá,
> que no es el propio manto y corona,
> que to huarache, que to huacal. (171)

> [*Amo quinequi, Juan Pamuceno,*
> don't place yourself as aristocrat
> 'cause it ain't proper the cloak and crown
> as is your sandals and your crate.]

In this stanza the parody of an Indian who speaks an awkward dialect is employed to remind Almonte of his inappropriate aspirations to establish a native aristocracy around a French court in a Mexican empire. Thus, the figure of Almonte is debased by his association with the symbols of Mexican unskilled workers—sandals and portable crates (*huarache* and *huacal*)—contrasted to those of the French nobility he favored: cloak and crown (*manto* and *corona*). Because the aristocratic norm is reversed on him, Almonte is portrayed as a satirized figure, incapable of truly attaining the qualities of a European (aristocratic = French) due to his inherently marginal attributes (plebeian = mestizo/Indian).

In this case a normative principle represented by Prieto and the Mexican intelligentsia defeats the party of the French interventionists, turning the comic representation of Almonte into punitive satire. Although Juan Nepomuceno Almonte was the son of José María Morelos y Pavón, one of the leaders of Mexican independence, had a brilliant military and diplomatic record, and possessed a refined culture and education, he is reminded that his racial background confines him to a marginal social and cultural status. Having Prieto, a patriot, defend the Mexican cause by satirizing Almonte's Indian origins reveals the extent to which the nineteenth-century liberal Mexican intelligentsia felt intimidated by European norms and embarrassed by the presence of Indian populations. The irony of Prieto's satiric attack is that it occurs during a nationalistic period in Mexican history and half a century after the declaration of independence from Spain.

Throughout the nineteenth century, Mexican authors parodied dialectal forms as a comic technique in the description of popular types who frequently mixed Nahuatl with Spanish. Although this practice is common in many Mexican genres—including normal discourse—the theater was a particularly suitable medium for this kind of verbal play, often involving satire.[31] Behind these verbal games lies the tendency toward the establishment of a cultural hegemony whose parameters have traditionally been dictated from Mexico City. These comic figures, however, were not always drawn from Mexican reality; often they were directly adapted from Spain. At the beginning of this century, Luis G. Urbina described how these peninsular borrowings took place:

> Se necesita ver bien para imitar bien. Los "aguadores" y "léperos" de nuestras revistas son interpretados con maestría entre nosotros; están al alcance de la observación de los artistas. . . . En cambio, en las piezas de marcado sabor español, en las costumbres populares madrileñas, vemos casi siempre torpeza y vacilación en alguno que otro cómico que no ha ido a España, y que por lo mismo no puede darse exacta cuenta del tipo, y adornarlo y bordarlo como quisiera, y como el autor lo ha concebido. (55)

> [You have to see precisely in order to imitate accurately. The "water-carriers" and "picaresque Mexican figures" of our revues are interpreted masterfully among us, they are within the reach of the artists. . . . But in the pieces of marked Spanish flavor, in the popular customs from Madrid, we generally see awkwardness and insecurity among some of the comics who have not gone to Spain and cannot, therefore, understand the type and provide it with the required style, the way the author has conceived it.]

The adaptation of popular types taken from Mexican daily life also took place in the regional theater of Yucatan in the years 1907 through 1926. During this period a number of dramatic representations portraying popular characters were made in zarzuelas (Spanish musical comedies), *sainetes* and *entremeses* (one-act farces), and *diálogos* (dialogues). The creations of this regional theater from southern Mexico included stereotyped figures such as the Turk, the Arab, the Chinese, the policeman, and the Indian and his young peasant girl, who employed a regional dialect as well as bilingual expressions (Magaña Esquivel 17). While in the popular theater of Yucatan some of these figures, especially the mestizo and the Indian, at first portrayed dignified characters, later on their function was circumscribed to comic or marginal roles.

Another example of the satirizing attitude toward figures representative of the rural culture appears in a manuscript belonging to a theatrical company active in Texas at the beginning of the present century. In a play entitled *Tenorio en solfa*—borrowing a scene from a zarzuela, or popular musical comedy ("Chin Chun Chan")—a rus-

tic husband-and-wife team demonstrate their amazement, as well as
their coarseness, upon their arrival in Mexico City.[32] As was customary in this type of comic portrayal, its humor was based on the
incongruity between the rural values of the couple and their reactions upon encountering the modern culture of the city. A Mexican
revue of the same period, "Las musas del país" (The national muses),
includes a similar scene. In its dialogue the town of Xochimilco (a
rural suburb of Mexico City at the time) is identified with the speakers' dialect. A comparison of both of these scripts allows us to trace
the process of adaptation of these rural figures into what will later
characterize the *pocho* and its feminine counterpart, the *pocha*. The
attitudes shown by the two couples in the dialogues reveal distinctive audience expectations: in the text from Mexico City, in addition to obvious references to local imagery, the Anglo-Americans are
mentioned in the role of tourists; while in the Texan (border) manuscript the verbal play assumes a certain familiarity with spoken English (*silki:* silk; *jotell:* hotel). In both dialogues, however, the use
of English is portrayed as a foreign language that provokes a comic
effect.

[El]   Si son de pura silqui como disen los gringos. . . .
[Ella]   A que tú tan pato pa que pidistis dos camas, olle se dise jotell.

[He: But they are of pure *silky*, as the gringos call them. . . .
She: Oh, you are so stupid, why did you ask for two beds, listen you say
HHHotel.] ([from Texas] Villalongín, *Tenorio en solfa*)

[Chema]   ¡Los gringos?
[Cleta]   Crioque sí. Esos siñores que parecían unos guamúchiles
           tiernos
[Chema]   ¡Ah! Pos esos meros son. Esos que lo decían "chichiscrais"
           y ponian el patota onde podían.

[Chema: The gringos?
Cleta: I think so. Those guys that looked like the tender *guamuchil*
tree.
Chema: Yea, they are the ones. They used to say "jesuschrist" and
would put their big feet wherever they could.] ([from Mexico City]
María y Campos, "Las musas del país" 147).

The Texan manuscript (*Tenorio en solfa*) includes characters that
parallel or anticipate the figure of the *pocho*. At an early stage in the
description of this process of cultural adaptation, the references to
the conflicts experienced by the Spanish-speaking population in the
United States played a secondary or minimal role. Later the *pocho*
and *pocha* came to portray negative figures whose comic behavior

served as an index of deviation from authentic or dignified Mexican cultural patterns.

These representations of non-European comic figures have profound implications for the formation of the cultural paradigm not only in Mexico but in the rest of the continent as well. It reveals the presence of conflictive normative values whereby Latin American national hegemonies based their values on Eurocentric aesthetics that practically relegated the majority of the native populations—and, consequently, their cultural expressions—to a status of marginality.[33] Thus, underlying the employment of indigenous expressions, regionalisms, and archaisms, as in the examples we have seen, lie the class conflicts caused by the racial and cultural mix that occurred during the colonial period. These examples among the mestizo and Creole groups of Mexico reveal the existence of controlling mechanisms that bar the social mobility of individuals with peasant or Indian racial and cultural traits. Thus, anyone identified with such background and who attempts to transgress the class barriers of this stratified society can expect to be automatically rebuffed. Satire is an effective and telling sign of how these mechanisms of cultural control operate, not only as instruments designed for the protection of the groups who maintain social and economic ascendancy but also as in-group devices that are internalized among the marginal.

The pocho

The term *pocho* appears as a publicly recognized label in Chicano books, newspapers, theatrical revues, and songs during the 1920s. Its usage assumes a tacit understanding of its meaning by a wide audience, thus suggesting its probable employment at an informal level for some time before.[34] Most of the evidence we have from this period is found in the immigrant press that flourished in the aftermath of the Mexican Revolution.[35] An early use of the term *pocho* appears associated with Californians whose cultural traits were judged to be heavily influenced by Anglo-American language and life-style. But it also was applied to individuals of Mexican rural origin who awkwardly imitated Anglo-American linguistic conventions. Arnold R. Rojas, discussing the language of Californians in the nineteenth century, suggests that the word may be of Indian origin: "About the only Indian word (said to be derived from the Yaqui—and that is debatable) is *pochi* or, lopped off or bob-tailed. A bob-tailed horse was called 'El Mocho' by Californians, and 'El Pocho' by Sonorans. Californians became 'pochos' or 'pochis' when Alta California was severed from Mexico" (20).[36]

In his *Cuentos Californianos*, published around 1922, Adolfo R. Carrillo (1865–1926) refers to the connotations of *pocho*, implying that the term was perceived then as a noun conveying distinct cultural characteristics (cited in Leal, *Aztlán y México* 112). In a description of the customers at a restaurant, Carrillo reveals that the word was used to identify a linguistic deviation from the norm: "[Ahí] se oyen todos los idiomas habidos y por haber, desde el gutural de los germanos, hasta el barbárico castellano que estropean los *pochos* Californianos." (There you may hear all the languages that may exist, from the guttural German, to the barbaric Castilian mishandled by the Californian *pochos*). A fuller treatment of *pocho* is found in the columns entitled "Crónicas diabólicas" by Jorge Ulica (Julio G. Arce) published in the newspaper *Hispano América* in San Francisco between 1916 and 1926. Thus, for example, in "Do You Speak Pocho?" "Los parladores de Spanish," and "No hay que hablar en pocho," Ulica satirizes the naive immigrant of rural origin who mixes Anglicisms with dialectal expressions and awkwardly adopts the customs of Anglo-Americans:

> El pocho se está extendiendo de una manera alarmante. Me refiero al dialecto que hablan muchos de los "spanish" que vienen a California y que es un revoltijo, cada día más enredado, de palabras españolas, vocablos ingleses, expresiones populares y terrible "slang."
> De seguir las cosas así, va a ser necesario fundar una Academia y publicar un diccionario español-pocho, a fin de entendernos con los nuestros. (*Crónicas diabólicas* 153)
>
> [*Pocho* is disseminating in a manner that causes alarm. I am referring to the dialect spoken by many of the "Spanish" that arrive in California and which consists of a mixture, every day more confusing, of Spanish words, English vocabulary, popular expressions, and awful "slang."
> Should things continue like this, it will become necessary to open a school and to publish a Spanish-Pocho dictionary in order to communicate with our own people.]

The term *pocho*, however, was more than a linguistic marker. It usually helped identify individuals of Mexican descent acculturated to Anglo-American ways and unable to express themselves according to the normative expectations of formal Spanish or to interact socially within Mexican groups. Speakers, therefore, employed the term in a wide range of usages. At one end of this semantic spectrum, it could simply acknowledge cultural differences, without pronounced animosity. This usage is evident in a song recorded in

1929, where the singer laments a flood that has brought misery both to "the Mexican and the Pocho:"

El martes, 13 de marzo
del novecientos veintiocho
es una fecha de luto
pa'l mexicano y pa'l pocho. ("Inundación of California")

[Tuesday, the thirteenth of March
of nineteen hundred and twenty-eight
is a day of mourning
for the Mexican and the Pocho.]

Another sense of the term, and decidedly satiric, is applied when vilifying individuals considered traitors to their own people and culture, ridiculing their adoption of Anglo-American traits.[37] This latter usage is readily apparent in a comic dialogue, recorded phonographically in 1937 ("La payasa: The Female Clown"), in which a Mexican male debates and ultimately defeats a *pocha*. The dialogue is a dispute involving gender, class, and Mexican nationality and opposing Anglo-American attitudes and customs. It is a contest in which the attacks of the male are centered on the female's pretense to pass as an American but who fails in her awkward attempts to conceal her Mexican origins:

Si por querer ser rubia a la fuerza piensa que la toman por gringa, lo que hace es ponerse en ridículo. . . . [E]s pura raza renegada. De las de que porque aquí compran trajes en abonos fáciles se creen la divina ganchuda, y ni hablar su idioma quieren . . . dió el primer peso de enganche y por el resto la andan buscando. Porque usted es de las que dice que cuesta menos cambiar de casa que pagar la renta.

[If wishing to be a blonde, by any means necessary, leads you to believe others will think you are a *gringa*, you are just making a fool of yourself. . . . You are the kind who betrays her own people. (You are of the kind) who buy new dresses on credit, believing themselves to be superior and then won't even speak their mother tongue. . . . you gave the first installment (on the merchandise) and now they are looking for you to pay the rest. You are the kind who believe it is easier to move away than to pay the rent.]

Throughout this debate a number of Mexican normative values are posed as superior to the false images available in American social, economic, and cultural life. The *pocha* is thus portrayed as someone who has traded one system of values for another without being able either to enter successfully into her adopted world or to erase her identification with the one she is abandoning. She is also accused of not being economically responsible, since it is unlikely that her clothes or rent are paid frequently, if at all—a veiled attack on the liberality of the American credit system that permits the adoption of a false class identity. The *pocha* is also stigmatized for adopting practices employed by American women, such as the use of hair dyes that permit them to become instant blonds. Her feminine beauty is thus claimed to be inherently false and, consequently, a distortion of the idealized figure of the beloved. In judging her under these norms, the male claims her as a compatriot, but his satirical description also carries a marked defensiveness toward the values he attacks, hence thwarting the comic effect. When this dialogue was recorded (1937)—a time of great economic difficulty due to the Great Depression and the forced repatriation of many Mexican immigrants—Chicanos were secure enough to resist these attempts to portray them comically. This dialogue is of interest because it demonstrates how violent antagonism or extreme bitterness on the part of an author transforms playful humor—usually associated in the portrayal of the comic figure of *pochos*—into invective. The dialogue is thus an illustration of how an author, feeling frustrated, may turn a comic target—perhaps inadvertently—into an object of satire.

Among Chicanos the comic or satirical usage of the term *pocho* may reflect the relationship between the speaker and the individual thus labeled. For example, at an intimate or familiar level an immigrant mother may address a daughter, affectionately, and somewhat teasingly with the diminutive *pochita*. Yet *pocho* may convey a derogatory meaning when employed toward a rival or an enemy. The term acquired yet a new sense in the novel *Pocho* by José Antonio Villarreal. Richard Rubio, Villarreal's hero-protagonist, portrays his ambivalence between upholding traditional Mexican cultural values and adopting the ways of the Anglo-American world in which he grows up. For Villarreal the word *pocho* is an in-group term used to describe the Chicano experience and is devoid of negative connotations, and in this sense his usage anticipates the role the term *Chicano* would acquire in the 1960s.[38] Because this work initiated a reassessment of Chicano historical reality that culminated during the 1960s and 1970s, scholars in Chicano studies rescued Villarreal's *Pocho* from oblivion and held it as a forerunner of the modern Chicano novel.[39]

The pachuco

The *pachuco* figure has been traced to a group of Chicano youths, living in El Paso in the early 1930s, whose language was heavily influenced by *caló*, the jargon of the Mexican underworld (Barker 191). According to this account, a court issued a judgment expelling a group of these youngsters from the city, some of whom opted to go to Los Angeles, where their influence spread and their elaborate dress, the zoot suit, along with their language, became a *pachuco* trademark.[40] But it was during the 1940s that the presence of *pachucos* became noticeable in practically every Chicano community as well as in Mexico.[41]

The community's feelings toward these individuals were often manifested through humor, and their language and unconventional behavior were frequently parodied. The depiction of the *pachuco* as a comic figure eventually became conventionalized to a few distinguishing features: an argot, a stylized zoot suit, and an unconventional behavior. Like the *pocho*, this figure became identified with individuals who violated the social and linguistic norms of Mexico and the United States. Unlike the *pocho*, however, the *pachuco* could also be a delinquent, an aspect that would be emphasized by his detractors. In addition, the *pachuco* was portrayed as a marginal urban inhabitant whose transgressions deformed the conventions of the Mexican working class.

In tracing the origins of the *pachuco*, Carlos Escudero, a journalist writing for *La Prensa* (San Antonio) in 1943, found a direct link between this new cultural expression and a figure that had existed in Mexico:

La manifestación de lo que algunos sociólogos ya llaman un fenómeno social tiene explicación relativamente sencilla. Los tipos del chaquetón son degeneración del gomoso, el petimetre, el pisaverde, el fifí de la capital Mexicana. ("El 'zoot suit'" 1)

[The expression of what some sociologists have already called a social phenomenon has a relatively simple explanation. Those individuals using the long coat are a deformation of the *gomoso, petrimetre, pisaverde,* and *fifí* (figures) from Mexico City.]

This observation, which suggests a direct relationship between the *pachuco* and the variants associated with the figure of the *fifí*, merits consideration. References to the *fifí* as a conventional figure are found throughout the literary and popular culture of Mexico during the nineteenth and early twentieth centuries. Antonio García Cubas in his *El libro de mis recuerdos* mentions some of the synonyms employed to identify this figure:

Los jóvenes a quienes se daban los diversos nombres de pisaverdes, currutacos, mequetrefes, dandys, petimetres, catrines y muy popular de rotos, vasta nomenclatura reducida hoy al nombre genérico de lagartijos, parábanse en las puertas y atrios de los templos para ver entrar y salir a las damas, en general, y cada cual, al objeto de su amor, en particular. (247)[42]

[The young people who received various names *pisaverdes, currutacos, mequetrefes, dandys, petimetres, catrines,* and *rotos,* multiple labels reduced nowadays to the generic *lagartijos* (lizards) would stand by the doors and atriums of the churches in order to see the entrance and exit of the ladies, in general, and each one, in particular, their object of love.]

Luis González Obregón, for his part, describes the *petimetres* from the beginning of the nineteenth century in what bears a distant resemblance to the exaggerated description of the zoot suiters some one hundred and thirty years later:

Los currutacos o petimetres en 1810 corrían parejos con las supradichas madamas [currutacas], por su calzado extravagante que a veces parecía lanceta y a veces barco veneciano; las medias detenidas con hebillas, a fin de no descubrir la falta de calzones; los pantalones cortos o largos, les nacían en los sobacos; las camisas o camisolitas, muy almidonadas y encarrujadas; los chupines, colgados de dijes; y los casacones o fraques, llegábanles hasta el tobillo, muy abotonados al pecho, pero tan angostos por la parte de atrás. (119)

[The *currutacos* or *petrimetres* in 1810 were similar to the abovementioned ladies (*currutacas*) because of their extravagant shoes which sometimes seemed a lancet, sometimes a Venetian boat; the stockings were held by buckles in order not to reveal the lack of underwear; the pants were short or long, and began in the armpits; the shirts or small blouses, quite starched and gathered; the underjacket full of hanging trinkets; and the overcoats would reach all the way to the ankle, quite buttoned to the chest, but so narrow in the back.]

A survival of this tradition is the *fifí* of the latter part of the nineteenth century and beginning of the twentieth. It must be pointed out that the *fifí* is a Spanish descendant of the dandy, a figure that emerged in England in the eighteenth century and that had a profound influence in European culture.[43] A broadside printed in 1918 by the editorial house of Vanegas Arroyo portrays the *fifí* in comic terms that coincide with those figures that later became known as the *pachucos:*

Los unos sin camisa
Los otros sin comer.
  Son los dandies
Fifís de actualidad
Terrible plaga

Que ha infestado
A toda la ciudad.
    Con One Step
Con exitación [sic]
Y el danzón
A muchas niñas
Han robado el corazón. ("Los fifís")

[Some without shirt
some without food
    The dandies
present-day fifís
are a plague that has infested
the whole city.
    With One Step
and excitement
and the danzón (type of dance)
they have robbed the heart
of many girls.]

A number of these qualities described are relevant to understanding the response *pachucos* were later accorded. The figure of the *fifí*, like that of the *pachuco*, is of a young man who shows a marked preference for new fashions in attire and dancing styles.[44] As flawed imitators of social etiquette, the *fifís* might be considered as minor social nuisances, hence comic figures, who presented no real threat to the established norms. The *pachucos* also were represented humorously, but became the objects of satire whenever perceived as a social menace. In both cases their image as fashionable urbanites is portrayed as hollow due to a poverty that bars them from successfully adopting the social roles vested on upper-class men.

The figure of the *fifí* was similar to its Anglo-American counterpart, the *jellybean*, another descendant of the dandy. The response of the Chicano community toward both *fifís* and *jellybeans* was often accompanied by a denunciation of their poor manners and their disruption of moral standards. In 1923 a news item in *La Prensa* (San Antonio) links both figures and commends the authorities during a campaign launched against them: "Magnífica es la campaña contra los 'fifís.'" (The campaign against the *fifís* is great.)

Son estos [fifís o jellybeans] individuos viciosos y atrevidos que careciendo de dignidad personal muchas veces juzgan que todo el mundo carece también de ella y así se dedican a la triste labor de importunar a cuanta mujer joven encuentran por las calles, invitándolas a "raids" y diciéndoles impudicias sin fijarse ni reparar en que se trate de señoras o señoritas honorables. . . .
    Para la estrecha mente de estos individuos no hay mujeres dignas y a

todas las tratan como si todas fueran de la calaña de "flappers" que desa-
fortunadamente abundan en la población. (1)

[These (*fifís* or *jellybeans*) are vice-ridden and shameless individuals
who, lacking personal dignity, assume that everyone else is the same;
they spend their time bothering every young woman whom they find in
the streets, inviting them for "raids" and making indecent commentaries, not caring whether they are addressing honorable single or married
ladies. . . .

In the narrow minds of these individuals, there are no respectable
women, and they treat all as "flappers," of whom, unfortunately, there
are many in this town.]

Pachucos were not often seen sympathetically by communities of
rural extraction who distrusted urban inhabitants and ridiculed the
fashions and life-styles of the city. An example of this attitude appears in the song "El rancho," recorded in 1926, where the superiority of rural ways is assumed, and its mockery of urban folk fore-
shadows the treatment later accorded to *pachucos*.

Por aquí todos con chico sacote
de atrás abierto hasta por aquí;
cuánto más valiera con chaqueta de hombre
como en el rancho donde yo nací.

[Around here everybody wears huge coats
with the back split up to here;
it'd be better a man's jacket,
just as it is used in the ranch where I was born.][45]

Twenty years later this trend will emerge as the zoot suit and become distinctly associated with *pachucos*. But urban Chicanos who
held deep respect for the etiquette of the bourgeoisie could only respond with disdain to the appearance of working-class youths dis-
torting the business suit. This is an attitude that appears in a detailed description of the *pachuco* suit made in the early 1940s by
one of the writers of *La Prensa* (San Antonio):

Visten un chaquetón de más de unas 37 pulgadas de largo, con tres bo-
tones de los cuales se usan los dos de arriba, hombros bien acolchados,
cintura recogida: 26 pulgadas de ancho de la pierna a la altura de la ro-
dilla, pero solamente 14 en el puño o valenciana del pantalón. El pantalón visto de sur a norte llega por lo general hasta cerca de las axilas del
bolsillo, pero del reloj cuelga una cadena que llega hasta las rodillas. (Escudero 1)

[They wear a jacket that is over 37-inches long, with three buttons of
which only two are used, the shoulders are heavily padded, the waist
is tight: the legs are 26-inches wide, but the pant cuffs measure only

14 inches. The pants, seen from north to south, generally go almost to
the armpit, but from the watch hangs a chain that reaches to the knees.]

Such a grotesque description of the *pachuco* suit is intended to
convey a deformation of its normative counterpart, the business
suit. In the description from *La Prensa,* this impression is achieved
by either gross exaggeration or else by minimizing the measure-
ments of various parts of the suit. Irony is conveyed by the pejorative
chaquetón (jacket), and distance is maintained through the playful
geographic reference "visto de sur a norte" (seen from north to
south). The result is of mock seriousness whereby the reader is
given a detailed explanation of the suit in terms resembling those of
a professional tailor, but with sufficient clues to warn the reader
that a fraudulent description is in progress. Yet the bourgeois norm
symbolized by the business suit is never debased, suggesting that for
the readers of *La Prensa* the fashions of urban clothing were symbols
of prestige.[46]
The life-style of the *pachucos* seems to have been widespread.
There are testimonies that this fashion also appeared among black
Americans and Filipinos.[47] A similar trend appeared among the marginal Argentines who danced the tango and among Cubans known
as *chucheros.* The description of the *chuchero* is of interest, since it
resembles that of the *pachuco,* suggesting that the phenomenon
represents an urban counterculture of working-class origins. The
chuchero had the following characteristics: he was of humble origins, smoked marijuana, wore a wide-brimmed hat, and wore two-
colored shoes made with goat skin, according to the tenets of his
African religious leanings. His pants were narrow, especially at the
cuffs, wide in the waist, and reached up to the chest. From the pants
hung a long chain which the *chuchero* continuously swung. The
coat reached almost to the knees and was square in the shoulders
which were padded in an exaggerated fashion, making him look ath-
letic. He wore his hair long on the sides and combed it constantly
(Sánchez-Boudy 10).
Perhaps the most influential source in the popularization of the
pachuco beyond the Chicano communities was the Mexican comic
Germán Valdés, "Tin Tan." In his film *El mariachi desconocido*
(1953), for example, "Tin Tan" demonstrates the close identification
that exists between the figures of the *pocho* and the *pachuco.* His
role is based on recurrent switches between these two figures—a
change that occurs whenever he receives a blow to the head, causing
a profound change in his personality. In his early portrayal of the
pachuco, "Tin Tan" emphasized language and clothing as central

to the figure. He thus represented the *pachuco* as an anti-hero of humble origins who led an unconventional existence. His comic depictions helped solidify the notion of social marginality and questionable behavior as fundamental traits of the *pachuco*. But the comedian appears to have exhausted this figure, since at a later stage in his career he abandoned almost all traces of his initial *pachuco* features.

The existence of the *pachucos* as violent figures became particularly noticeable beyond the confines of the Chicano communities during World War II, when Anglo-American sailors had violent confrontations with Mexican youths, identified in English-language newspapers as "zoot suiters." In his perceptive study of these riots, Mauricio Mazón points out the polarized situation this confrontation created inside and outside the Chicano communities:

> So intense and pervasive was the imagery of destruction during the riots that it was difficult for the press, law enforcement officials, and even some of the participants to distinguish between symbolic and physical actions. The predominant view was of several hundred gangs of zoot-suiters unleashed from the barrio and bent on destroying the life of the city. Within the Mexican-American community a similar view prevailed, except that the threat was perceived in terms of gangs of servicemen (and in some cases policemen) who were randomly roving the streets hunting for zoot-suiters. (Mazón 112)

Thus, the role of the *pachuco* becomes ambivalently associated with images of urban juvenile delinquents prone to violence or else as the victims of racial paranoia. Mazón describes how the figure of the *pachuco* was interpreted in negative terms within the American mainstream during a period of national emergency when: "Fantasies of martial prowess, of physically cleansing the country of undesirable elements, and of annihilating zoot-suiters could do much to alleviate ambivalent feelings about war and to assuage moods of dissatisfaction and ennui" (Mazón 52).

The image of *pachucos* as social undesirables is also evident in the views expressed by Mexicans. In his introductory essay to *El laberinto de la soledad,* Octavio Paz refers to them as portraying "un dandismo grotesco y de una conducta anárquica" (a grotesque dandyism and a anarchistic behavior) explaining their existence as a desperate response: "No han encontrado más respuesta a la hostilidad ambiente que esta exagerada afirmación de su personalidad" (They have not found other response to the hostility of their environment than the exaggerated affirmation of their personalities) (13–14). As an outsider who observed *pachucos* during a short stay in Los Angeles, Paz measures them according to Mexican norms and concludes, "Queramos o no, estos seres son mexicanos, uno de los extremos a que puede llegar el mexicano" (Whether we like it or not, these human beings are Mexican, one of the extremes the Mexican may reach). In his characterization of the *pachuco*, Paz suggests that the loss of Mexican culture has brought on an irrational or disorderly system of values that has produced this figure:

> Cuando se habla con ellos [los mexicanos de Los Angeles] se advierte que su sensibilidad se parece a la del péndulo, un péndulo que ha perdido la razón y que oscila con violencia y compás. Este estado de espiritu—o de ausencia de espiritu—ha engendrado lo que se ha dado en llamar el "pachuco." (13)

> [When one speaks with them (Mexicans in Los Angeles), it is noticeable that their sensibility seems like a pendulum, a pendulum that has no reason and oscillates violently like a compass. This state of the spirit— or lack of spirit—has generated what has been called the *pachuco*.]

In *Laberinto* the *pachucos* are no longer comic figures: "El pachuco es un clown impasible y siniestro, que no intenta hacer reir y que procura aterrorizar" (The *pachuco* is an impassive and sinister clown, who does not intend to produce laughter but who tries to terrorize) (15). It is perhaps no coincidence that, in this renowned study of Mexican culture, the *pachuco* occupies the first chapter and that this "extreme" would represent a threat to Mexican culture. During the postrevolutionary and postwar years, an emerging Mexican middle class was in the process of consolidating an official version of Mexican culture, and the presence of Chicanos in the United States represented a "shameful" reminder of a history (1848) and a class (*braceros*) that did not serve them well in their aspirations as a developing Western nation. Paz is a spokesman for this class.[48]

From an in-group perspective, Mexican Americans would express a similar view toward *pachucos*. For the returning veterans—armed with pride in their decorated war heroes, their military services' loans and scholarships, and newly acquired skills that enabled them to obtain jobs away from farms and barrios—the presence of *pachucos* was a bitter reminder of a past they felt had been left behind. Thus, Manuel Servín derided the *pachucos* for their un-Mexican behavior and their outlandish dress and blamed them for projecting a group image of "lawlessness, cowardice, and disloyalty," lamenting the effect this blot caused on the Chicano communities' image, undermining "the hard-earned reputation of prewar Mexicans": "As a result, the heroic service of the Mexican-Americans in the Philippines as well as the outstanding bravery of the proportionally numerous Medal of Honor winners were ignored by the North American whites and blacks" (168).

This response, blaming the zoot suiters for the discredit they brought on the positive image of Mexicans, was predictable from those sectors of the communities—that is, immigrants and Mexican Americans—that had struggled to solve community problems exclusively in terms of Mexican or Anglo-American cultural strategies.[49] Mazón points out that as a result the "zoot-suiters were rendered ahistorical, anomalous, having no place in the past or future of either Mexico or the United States" and that "the only legitimate scholarly recourse was to discredit barrio youth" (Mazón 116–117).

Although the views toward the *pachucos* had been polarized within and outside the Chicano community—as had been the case with the *pochos*—it is evident that some observers could already assess their existence beyond an either/or normative focus. Thus, the organization of the Sleepy Lagoon Defense Committee in support of the youths accused in the "zoot suit murders" represented, in the words of its chairman, Carey McWilliams, "the first well-organized and widely supported effort in Southern California to bring the case of the Mexican, or the citizen of Mexican descent, to the attention of all the peoples of the area" (Endore 3). This was also a view that signaled the possibility of researching the Chicano experience as an expression of firmly rooted social and historical conditions. These efforts may be seen as important antecedents to the model that eventually emerged during the 1960s. In this latter conception, Chicanos would be a principal focus rather than solely incidental or ancillary phenomena deforming normative hegemonic values.

It is not coincidental that two prominent figures in Chicano culture, the *pocho* and the *pachuco*, became the subject of special attention in the 1960s. Both figures have represented symbolic aspects of the Chicano experience and, during this period of critical introspection, were subjected to a radical revaluation. Although the meaning of the term *pocho* has had diverse connotations over the years, its primary meaning is of an individual of Mexican descent who resides in the United States, belongs to the working class, is of rural background, and whose language and customs show a marked degree of Anglo-American cultural influence.[50] The meaning of the term *pachuco*, on the other hand, is more specific, since it conveys a style of dress, the use of underworld slang, and an unorthodox stance toward the norms both within and without the Chicano community.[51]

As in the case of other nomenclature used in relation to Chicanos, the meaning of the terms *pocho* and *pachuco*—which also function as subgroup nicknames—depends on a variety of factors that may include the intent of the speaker, the identity of the addressee, and the context in which it is used. From the perspective of many Anglo-Americans, both of these figures became stereotypical for all Chicanos, while in Mexico *pochos* and *pachucos* were perceived as a distortion of the norms of Mexican culture and hence subjected to censure. In this sense both may be considered as related figures.

> For many Mexicans the pachuco represented the crystallization of the *pocho*, i.e., a Mexican born in the United States; alien to both cultures; fluent in neither Spanish nor English; a specialist in Caló, the argot of lumpen elements—an ideal subject for ethnocentric apologies or chauvinistic attacks. In Mexico the pachuco was perceived as a caricature of the American, while in the United States the pachuco was proof of Mexican degeneracy. (Mazón 5)

Within Chicano communities, however, these figures were easily identifiable and judged—sympathetically by some, harshly by others. Many community members were familiar with cultural borrowing and were thus not offended by the use of Anglicisms, the blending of conventions, or the wearing of the zoot suit. In other sectors of the community, however, *pochos* and *pachucos* represented a deformation of traditional norms: some saw them as comic figures, while others considered them an embarrassment. Since Chicano acculturation runs along a continuum that extends from a Mexican to an Anglo-American extreme, the degree of *pochismo* or *pachuquismo* was variable and could be perceived from a wide range of perspectives.

Although the term *pachuco* shares characteristics with the label *pocho*, a significant difference between the two rests in the restricted meaning of the former and the general applicability of the latter. In other words, although both expressions may be used as exclusionary labels—capable of conveying a range of meanings of varied affective connotations—*pachuco* has also an in-group, or subgroup, meaning. As in the case of any other social affiliation, *pachucos* maintain a set of hierarchical codes that determine prestige and ascendancy, a sense of pride in the characteristics associated with the group, as well as a certain disdain for those extraneous to their membership (Barker 191). Yet a fundamental distinction exists between the sociological and historical reality of these two figures and their folkloric or literary characterizations.[52] It is this latter aspect, the representational dimensions of the *pocho* and the *pachuco* as comic and satirical figures within the confines of the communities of Mexican descent in the United States, that has been relevant to our present purpose.

2. Luis Valdez and *Actos* of Teatro Campesino

Luis Valdez was a young drama graduate in 1965 when he decided to join the United Farmworkers Organizing Committee (UFWOC) led by César Chávez in Delano, California. His decision was guided by a political and artistic vision: creating a popular theater that would serve as support to the organizational activities of the striking farmworkers. In addition to his academic preparation, Valdez had worked with the San Francisco Mime Troupe, where he gained valuable experience in translating controversial social issues into political theater. Valdez knew firsthand the issues involved in the labor dispute: he was born in Delano, and his family still resided in the area after spending many years as migratory farmworkers. He was thus especially sensitive to the different conflictive responses *La Huelga* (The strike) would elicit in the surrounding Chicano communities. This extraordinary combination of formal training, practical experience, and intimate knowledge of farmworker culture proved to be a most valuable foundation in the development of El Teatro Campesino.[1]

Valdez faced difficult conditions to establish the Teatro Campesino. The headquarters of the UFWOC had no staging facilities; the majority of cast members were volunteers, most without previous acting experience; and the audience engaged in a lively, sometimes chaotic interaction with the performers. Furthermore, the attention of the striking members of the UFWOC was directed principally at the strikebreakers, the ranch owners who resisted signing contracts, and the ever-threatening presence of the local police. Valdez has described the beginnings of El Teatro Campesino as an immediate emotional response of the farmworkers to the incidents occurring at the picket line:

> The first huelguista [striker] to portray an esquirol [scab] in the Teatro did it to settle a score with a particularly stubborn scab he had talked with in the fields that day. Satire became a weapon that was soon aimed at known and despised contractors, growers and *mayordomos*. The ef-

fect of those early *Actos* on the huelguistas de Delano packed into Filipino Hall was immediate, intense, and cathartic. The *Actos* rang true to
the reality of the Huelga. (*Actos* 5)

Comic and Satiric Figures

An immediate source for Valdez was the agitprop theater and the
epic theater of Bertold Brecht; Valdez received both of these influences from the San Francisco Mime Troupe and the Bread and Puppet Theater. This theatrical indebtedness, however, does not indicate a direct or indiscriminate borrowing of plots or individual
characters. In order to appeal to an audience of farmworkers, Valdez
adapts motifs, character traits, and dramatic strategies that conform
to relevant aspects of Mexican folk culture. Significant in this regard
is the linguistic authenticity of the *Actos,* in which the everyday
speech of Chicanos is introduced, including code switching between
Spanish and English, and the use of dialectal forms that mix archaisms, regionalisms, and *caló* (underworld slang).[2] This popular orientation was central in the naming of the *Actos:*

> Even the name we gave our small presentations reflects the hard press-
> ing expediency under which we worked from day to day. We could have
> called them "skits," but we lived and talked in San Joaquin Valley Span-
> ish (with a strong Tejano influence) so we needed a name that made
> sense to the Raza. Cuadros, pasquines, autos, entremeses all seemed too
> highly intellectualized. We began to call them *Actos* for lack of a better
> word, lack of time and lack of interest in trying to sound like classical
> Spanish scholars. (*Actos* 5–6)

Some important characteristics of his antitraditionalist stance
may be ultimately traced to dramatic tradition, particularly to Roman comedy. Valdez acknowledged this classical influence, pointing
out some ironic parallels with his own experience: "There are certain people that appeal to me, I think of them as Chicanos. Plautus,
for instance, the Roman playwright, who used to be a slave and
wrote comedies. . . . I liked the fact that he was a slave that became
a playwright. That's me!" (Hernández, "Interview with Luis Valdez"). Indeed, a number of parallels may be drawn between the *Actos* and Plautine comedy, including the relationship between masters and servants, the use of exaggeration, buffoonery, and sexual
humor, as well as the portrayal of conflicts involving money, morals,
and intricate social loyalties.[3] Some of the ancient figures that
evolved during the Renaissance also captured Valdez' imagination:

"The cunning slave is one of the classic figures; [it] starts with the Greeks, goes into the Romans, goes into the Renaissance; is [evident] throughout" (Hernández, "Interview with Valdez").

In addition to this acquaintance with classical Greek and Roman drama, Valdez received the influence of authors such as Tirso de Molina and Moliere, whose wily servants are re-created in the *Actos* in the figure of the *coyote* and the *esquirol* (scab). He associates the character of the boastful soldier *(miles gloriosus)*—that is, the figure of Falstaff in Shakespeare—with some of the figures in the *Actos*, including the deceitful attitude displayed by false student militants and corrupt, dishonest ranchers. The works of the English dramatist Ben Jonson made Valdez aware of the Italian commedia dell'arte. In the birth of the *Actos*, then, there is a merging of learned and popular traditions.[4]

A significant example of the syncretic nature of Teatro Campesino is found in the portrayal of the labor contractor *(el contratista)*, or Don Coyote. This is a traditional trickster figure who flatters his masters while he displays ingenuous resourcefulness and callous self-interest. In the *Actos* this character borrows from the coyote figure of Hispanic folklore and the classical figure of the wily servant (see Meléndez 301). The figure of Don Coyote is an artistic response to both the external and the internal factors that have molded the social and psychological experience of Chicanos. But actual labor conditions were the direct inspiration for the figure of the contractor in his role as a parasitic and opportunistic middleman:

> The farm labor contractor is one of the most hated figures in the entire structure of agri-business. He is paid by the growers for having the special skill of rounding up cheap stoop labor in the barrio and delivering it to the fields. The law stipulates that he must provide safe transportation and honest transaction. The sorrowful reality is something else again, ranging from broken down buses that are carbon monoxide death traps to liquor and meager lunches sold at exorbitant prices to the workers. In the field, Don Coyote sits in his air-conditioned pickup while the workers suffer the blistering heat or freezing cold of inclement weather. (*Actos* 21)

The representation of Don Coyote provided the Teatro Campesino with rich dramatic possibilities. His role was a blend, in parodic fashion, of the privileged status of the rancher and that of the subservient and exploited farmworker. But the tension thus created avoids the danger—inherent in all satire—of becoming repetitive or exhausting the themes of victimization and oppression. Indeed, relentless satirical attack on ranchers may easily tire audiences painfully familiar with the callous attitude of landowners, and the continual derision of scabs (strikebreakers) might alienate nonstriking farmworkers and hinder the proselytizing efforts of the union.

Don Coyote's transformation from a folk figure into a humanized character draws from another important tradition: the picaresque. Valdez, however, inverts the conventional trait of the picaro as "half-outsider," into what may appropriately be referred to as "half-insider."[5] That is, whereas the picaresque anti-hero is portrayed, comically, as an outsider who fails in his attempt to enter a higher social group, the *contratista*-coyote is perceived, satirically, as failing in his attempt to abandon his peers. This emphasis on *insideness* over *outsideness* is fundamental in the interpretation of many Chicano literary texts whose protagonists, as marginal minorities, confront hegemonic barriers that impede their self-realization.

The values of Don Coyote represent a satire on aspiring Chicanos who seek personal advancement while rejecting their cultural and community ties. His function is to provide a negative model opposed to an implicit normative figure represented by the honest Chicano who maintains loyalty to the community. In many of the *Actos*, Valdez is critical of mainstream adverse attitudes internalized by some Chicanos. Valdez thus shifts his denunciation from external factors that foil the struggles of Chicanos to internal, questionable values that cause unscrupulous behavior. Self-defeat is portrayed by two types of characters: (1) oppressive figures who profit through the exploitation of Chicanos who are in weak or vulnerable positions and (2) victimized figures who foolishly accept conditions that are denigrating. Don Coyote is a comic figure who illustrates how internal and external factors help shape the social and psychological experience of Chicanos.

Las dos caras del Patroncito

In this, the first published *acto* of Teatro Campesino, Valdez already includes some of his favorite dramatic techniques, such as the use of masks, the portrayal of ludicrous characters, plot reversals, and jesting dialogues. The plot of *Las dos caras* is based on a simple inversion of roles: determined to realize his wish to be a Mexican worker, a wealthy and powerful landowner (Patroncito) orders one of the strikebreakers he has hired (Farmworker) to trade identities with him. After exchanging masks—a symbolic representation of fate's whimsical assignment of social roles—the landowner, deprived of his privileged status, understands firsthand the injustices suffered by agricultural laborers and becomes an ardent supporter of

César Chávez and the striking farmworkers.[6] This reversal of roles is conventional in the Western tradition and is usually employed to depict a sudden loss of triumph or privilege. Such changes usually indicate a personal and social crisis that tests individual character. In the *acto*, however, this transformation involves the arbitrary ascent of the farmworker and the descent of Patroncito toward opposite ends of their respective hierarchical status. It subverts the notion that social identity and evaluating frameworks are the result of personal choice, since, as these two protagonists demonstrate, values depend on the fortuitous circumstances of birth.

A sense of irony is evident in the choice of the protagonist's name: Patroncito. The term *patrón* has a variety of meanings, ranging from admiration and respect, to fear, and even hatred, depending upon the context in which it is employed and the intentions of the speaker. By attaching the diminutive ending *cito*, Valdez highlights the ambiguity of the noun and its connotations of admiration or dislike. It is this latter derogatory usage and context that is conveyed by the name Patroncito, and the subservience of the scab when thus addressing his boss renders the worker a subject of ridicule to the audience of striking farmworkers. Throughout the *acto* the implicit authorial voice assumes the role of arbiter and invites the audience to share in unmasking (literally and figuratively) the contradictions that inform the social injustice represented by the figure of the Patroncito and the internalization of servile attitudes on the part of the scab farmworker.

In spite of his newly enlightened perspective, Patroncito ultimately reveals the false values that underlie his oppressive behavior. The duality conveyed by Patroncito's having "two faces" reveals his unredeeming hypocrisy: he is arrogant when wielding power but rebellious when experiencing the unjust treatment accorded to his workers. His moral delusion is only defensible from the perspective of the corrupt—that is, ranchers and apologists for the agricultural lobby who oppose the striking farmworkers. Only a distorted sense of reality can justify Patroncito's belief that rural poverty is a pastoral existence free from tax burdens and the great expenses besieging the wealthy. His envy and wish to live the life of a Mexican worker is grounded on such fallacy:

[PATRONCITO] Just one of my boys. Riding in the trucks, hair flying in the wind, feeling all that freedom, coming out here to the fields, working under the green vines, smoking a cigarrete, my hands in the cool soft earth, underneath the blue skies, with white clouds drifting by, looking at the mountains, listening to the birdies sing.
[FARMWORKER] (ENTRANCED) I got it good. (*Actos* 14)

The incongruity of this parody of the ideal landscape is compounded by the comic figure of Patroncito frivolously trading his identity with the laborer. He is thus the protagonist of a mock epic in which foolishness, not blinding pride (hubris), causes his absurd downfall. To an audience of farmworkers, who know the dehumanized conditions confronted daily in the fields, the debasement of the figure represented by Patroncito was an important turning point in the assertion of their dignity.

Maintaining the goals pursued by the UFWOC, the Teatro Campesino addressed the improvement of salaries and working conditions of the farmworkers. This purpose is evident in the closing scene of the play where the farmworker decides to keep Patroncito's cigar but disregards the possibility of seizing either the rancher's property or power. Although the UFWOC and the Teatro were often accused of communist sympathies, the comic ending painstakingly avoids a possible Marxist denouement where the workers would take possession of the rancher's property, signaling a proletariat triumph over their capitalist oppressors.[7] The truly heroic figure implicit in this *acto* is the farmworker who demands a rightful compensation and has joined the strike with dignity and moral resolve.

Los vendidos

In 1967, in a most significant decision, the Teatro Campesino separated from the UFWOC and moved to a new location in Del Rey, California, and a new beginning as an independent company.[8] This turning point in Valdez' career allowed for new dramatic possibilities, since the Teatro could now expand its audience as well as incorporate new themes, characters, and plots in their performances. *Los vendidos* illustrates how the company met this challenge. First performed at Elysian Park in East Los Angeles before a gathering of the Brown Berets, a group of Chicano community activists, the *acto* addresses a young urban Chicano audience concerned with sociopolitical issues. Adapting themes previously employed—such as the praise of in-group solidarity and the denunciation of personal success when it entails materialism and cultural disloyalty—the satiric target of this *acto* focuses on the stereotypical images of Chicanos. The Teatro's audiences responded enthusiastically to the dramatization of some of their innermost conflicts involving social identity, now portrayed openly and unapologetically. El Teatro Campesino thus emerged as a vital arm in a Chicano movement of cultural affirmation.

Los vendidos, following the Teatro's characteristic dramatic techniques, includes a deceptively simple plot, ingenious humorous episodes, and a surprising reversal of events for its closure. The setting is at Honest Sancho's Used Mexican Lot and Mexican Curio Shop, a title that suggests both the dishonesty associated with the sale of secondhand cars and the banality of the Mexican arts and crafts sold to tourists. To Honest Sancho's shop arrives Miss Jimenez (spelled "JIM-enez," mocking an English pronunciation of her name), who has come to purchase a Mexican type to serve in "Governor Reagen's office." Sancho, its proprietor, manager, and salesman, describes the several models he has in stock.[9] Miss Jimenez finds the first few models unsuitable, as the farmworker is unpolished, the revolutionary is unable to speak English, and the *pachuco* is a delinquent. Her requirements are met by the Mexican-American model whose linguistic and social assimilation she judges to be appropriate for a role in state government.[10] After she has concluded her purchase, however, the Mexican-American model develops a "dysfunction" and begins to voice antiestablishment statements. He is joined by the other models, forcing the frightened Miss Jimenez hurriedly to depart from the shop. In a final scene, the audience discovers that the models are in fact real people acting out stereotypical roles, whereas Honest Sancho is only a mannequin that must be carried out at the end of the performance.[11]

The creation of the characters of Honest Sancho, a former labor contractor, and Miss Jimenez, a Mexican American, represents a variation of such earlier figures as the Coyote and the scab. These are figures who personify traits considered detrimental to Chicanos and who are essentially mediating parasites who operate between the Chicano and the Anglo communities. The name Sancho is associated in popular speech with the lover of a married woman and has a series of connotations ranging from the tragic to the comic, depending on its context.[12] These meanings are not likely to escape the audience who would also respond skeptically to someone with "Honest" as a name. Indeed, Sancho is a figure who, taking advantage of the weak socioeconomic position of other Chicanos, profits by manipulating their negative images in Anglo-American society—an extension of his previous role when, as a labor contractor, he capitalized on their work.

The figure of Sancho has as counterpart the ridiculous Miss Jimenez, a character blending the traditional image of the *pocha* with the emerging Mexican-American middle class. Within this context Miss Jimenez represents a level of assimilation into the U.S. mainstream that makes her a virtual stranger to her own culture and people, whereas Sancho is still socially and culturally indistinguishable from other Chicanos. Both figures, however, demonstrate their complicity—one as an agent of the out-group, the other as an in-group member—in the support and exploitation of stereotypical images that are antithetical to the well-being of Chicanos. Ironically, these deviants, Sancho and Miss Jimenez, are figures who might otherwise be considered as role models for Chicanos in the eyes of Anglo-American society. The two figures portray variations on a salient theme that informs Valdez' early work and which may be formulated as follows: given the sociocultural conflicts encountered by Mexicans living in the United States, their only viable ethical conduct is to maintain loyalty toward their own group in spite of the overwhelming external pressures to turn against their own.

Los vendidos is the *acto* that has probably been most often performed by other Chicano theater companies (Huerta 61–62). This success lies, undoubtedly, in the ridicule the play directs toward portrayal of Chicanos as stereotypical figures. *Los vendidos* demonstrates how social restrictions reduce Chicano cultural variability to a series of comic figures. Valdez satirizes these representational types, but he vents his wit primarily on those individuals who are able to perceive Chicanos only in farcical terms. In a single stroke, he also synthesizes a problem causing great tension within the Chicano psyche: the contradictions of internalizing the normative values of a dominant group that relegates them to a status of marginality—denying prestige to Chicanos who assert their cultural background while rewarding those who demonstrate social and cultural disloyalty. The importance of this *acto*, therefore, cannot be overemphasized: it marks a historic turning point in Chicano self-perception.

In satirizing the false image of Chicanos, Valdez employs a narrative structure that resembles a Menippean type of dialogue, *Philosophies for Sale,* written by the Greek satirist Lucian of Samosata (A.D. 120?). Both *Los vendidos* and *Philosophies for Sale* involve the public sale of individuals who represent specific social traits. In the ancient dialogue, Hermes, the Greek god of trade, auctions various philosophical positions (a Pythagorean, a Cynic, a Cyrenaic, a Democritean, a Heraclitean, an Academic, a Stoic, a Peripatetic, and a Skeptic), whereas in the *acto* the characters sold by Honest Sancho are representative of Chicano stereotypes (a farmworker, a revolutionary, a *pachuco*, and a Mexican American). In both representations the human merchandise is displayed comically. Although the figures reflect contemporary values, they are characterized in exaggerated terms. It is an absurdity further compounded when some of the prospective buyers feel reluctant to pay the prices asked for certain models.

Especially notable are the parallels between the figures of the Cynic and the *pachuco*. The unconventional behavior advocated by the Cynic summarizes those views presenting the *pachuco* life-style in negative terms:

> [CYNIC] You should be impudent and bold, and should abuse all and each, both kings and commoners, for thus they will admire you and think you manly. Let your language be barbarous, your voice discordant and just like the barking of a dog: let your expression be set, your gait consistent with your expression. In a word, let everything about you be bestial and savage. Put off modesty, decency and moderation, and wipe away blushes from your face completely. (Lucian 469)

The *pachuco* displays these traits of male abusiveness, uncouth language, and affected gestures and body movements. Sancho describes him as an expert on urban survival, particularly through the use of violence, and proceeds to demonstrate the model's behavior. In a slapstick scene, Johnny pulls out his switchblade and swings at the retreating Miss Jimenez, who screams in horror (40).

The eccentrically frugal life advocated by the Cynic parallels the comically modest upkeep Johnny Pachuco will cause his purchaser:

> [SANCHO] Nickels and dimes. You can keep Johnny running on hamburgers, Taco Bell tacos, Lucky Lager beer, Thunderbird wine, yesca. (*Actos* 41)

> [CYNIC] Next I will compel you to undergo pains and hardships, sleeping on the ground, drinking nothing but water and filling yourself with any food that comes your way. (Lucian 467)

In both cases this deprivation includes physical torture:

> [CYNIC] . . . and if anyone flogs you or twists you on the rack, you will think that there is nothing painful in it. (Lucian 467)

> [SANCHO] He [Pachuco] can also be beaten and he bruises, cut him and he bleeds, kick him and he . . . He is a great scapegoat . . . Why, the LAPD [Los Angeles Police Department] just bought 20 of these to train their rookie cops on. (*Actos* 41–42)

In one Lucianic scene, Hermes reassures a fearful buyer to disregard the frightening appearance of the Cynic:

[BUYER] I am afraid of his sullen, hang-dog look; he may bark at me if I go near him, or even bite me, by Zeus!
[HERMES] Don't be afraid; he is gentle. (Lucian 463)

A similar conclusion is reached in the *acto* by the secretary after Sancho has encouraged her to test the physical resiliency of Johnny Pachuco:

[SECRETARY] Well, alright. Just once. (SHE KICKS PACHUCO) Oh, he's so soft. (*Actos* 42)

Other philosophies ridiculed by Lucian find parallels in Valdez' *acto*. For example, the Revolutionary and/or Early California Bandit type share features with the Cyrenaic:

[HERMES] In general, he is accommodating to live with, satisfactory to drink with and profligate master when he riots about town with a flute girl. (Lucian 473)

[SANCHO] Another feature about this one [revolutionary] is that he is economical. He runs on raw horsemeat and tequila!
[SECRETARY] Isn't that rather savage?
[SANCHO] Al contrario it makes him a lover. (*Actos* 43)

The final model offered by Sancho, the Mexican American, shares a number of significant elements with the peripatetic philosopher. Both are knowledgeable, expensive, and have a dual nature.

[HERMES] (TO PERIPATETIC) I say, you who are handsome, you who are rich! (TO THE BUYERS) Come now, buy the height of intelligence, the one who knows absolutely everything!
[BUYER] What is he like!
[HERMES] Moderate, gentlemanly, adaptable in his way of living, and, what is more, he is double . . . Viewed from the outside, he seems to be one man, and from the inside, another; so if you buy him, be sure to call the one self "exoteric" and the other "esoteric." (Lucian 503)

[SANCHO] Ain't he a beauty? Feast your eyes on him! Sturdy US Steel frame, streamlined, modern. As a matter of fact, he is built exactly like our Anglo models except that he comes in a variety of darker shades: naughahide, leather, or leatherette . . . Yes, señorita, this model represents the apex of American engineering! He is bilingual, college educated, ambitious! Say the word "acculturate" and he accelerates. He is intelligent, well-mannered . . . (*Actos* 44–45)

The similarities between Lucian's dialogue and Valdez' *acto* may be solely a literary coincidence. Valdez does not recall reading Lucian and, when asked to comment on a possible Lucianic influence on his work, replied that should such borrowing from the Greek author have occurred it would have been "perhaps at a subconscious level."[13] It is probable that the resemblances between the dialogue and the *acto* may have arisen from the employment of similar characters and social settings. After all, in the ancient world, the marketplace was a center of life, and slavery had ramifications into virtually every aspect of society. Similarly, the car industry is a fundamental factor in modern American society. In satirizing philosophers Lucian employed a marginal figure, the slave trader, whose function was considered as disreputable in antiquity as the used-car salesman is in our times (Wiedemann 6; Konstan 31). Given this initial coincidence in setting and plot, the employment of traditional comic figures by Valdez produced a resemblance between the two dramatic pieces—that is, in the mocking of poverty, food, and dress, the drinking and carousing, or in the presence of characters with "dual" or incongruous personalities. In other words, the characters coincide because in the representation of these figures there is a distortion of positive normative values, that is, frugality, courage, love, wisdom, strength, and so forth. These parallels between Lucian and Valdez may actually demonstrate how the stock repertoire of literary and popular figures is easily adaptable to diverse chronological and cultural settings as well as to a variety of ideological persuasions.

No sacó nada de la escuela

The *acto No sacó nada* is addressed to an audience composed primarily of students at high schools, colleges, and universities. Its title (literally: "He didn't get anything out of school") is a Mexican colloquialism used as a derogatory expression when referring to individuals who, having attended school, are lacking either in knowledge, manners, or judgment. It is an expression generally employed to censure the learner for failing to uphold the positive normative characteristics of the educated. But in the *acto*, this expression is employed sarcastically, since it is the teaching institution that is censured for failing the student. It is a criticism directed to the insensitivity of schools toward the educational needs of Chicano children.[14] Thus, in *No sacó nada*, American education is the object of attack—Valdez' most pointed satire in the *actos*; and the teachers' prejudices are portrayed as the most formidable social barrier facing Chicano students.

The importance of *No sacó nada* lies in its treatment of events from the perspective of Chicano children who enter an alien educational world. The focus on childhood has been conventional in contemporary Chicano literature. In many Chicano creative works, young children or adolescents are portrayed as undergoing painful experiences in the transition from the support and familiarity of their homes and communities to the foreign and sometimes unsympathetic world of U.S. social institutions.[15] While initiation into a school environment may pose a difficult transition for most children, for Chicanos it can be a traumatic experience due to the cultural conflicts it often entails, that is, an abrupt change in language, values, and attitudes. Valdez focuses on this theme while subjecting the teachers, the school system, and U.S. society to his satire.

The *acto* dramatizes this criticism by following the experience of a group of students through their attendance in elementary school, high school, and college. The students represent a variety of characteristics that include class, race, and culture, and their interaction is portrayed as a grotesque microcosm of U.S. social relations. Accordingly, the classroom socialization of youth is a process of acculturation whereby teachers reinforce the biased divisions and class structures that exist in U.S. society. This censure of educational institutional practices coincided with a period of generational rebellion by American youth that has been unparalleled in U.S. history. But Chicano groups adhered to the belief that their social and economic advancement depended on a better education. Thus, *No sacó nada* is important as a Chicano satirical text because it posits education as a central factor in liberating Chicanos from their status of marginality.

A central character in the play, Francisco, is the object of abuse and isolation in school as punishment for demonstrating cultural loyalty to his community. Francisco serves as an exemplary character while his antithesis, Monty (Moctezuma), as a prototype of the Mexican American, rejects his own culture while vainly seeking the acceptance of the white middle-class fellow students and teachers. Another significant character is Esperanza, who undergoes a radical transformation: from being a feminine counterpart to Moctezuma, in her caricatured portrayal of the Mexican American, to a position where she becomes a socially conscious Chicana. In naming these figures, Valdez follows his practice of portraying characters that represent types or roles. Thus, Francisco's rebelliousness is inspired by the Mexican revolutionary hero Francisco Villa, a revered figure for many Chicanos and the subject of an earlier play by Valdez, *The Shrunken Head of Pancho Villa* (Huerta 49–60). Moctezuma, a name Valdez had employed in *La conquista de México* (*Actos*

50–65), evokes the figure of the Aztec emperor who surrendered to the Spaniards and is used here as a symbol of weakness. The name Esperanza (Hope) clearly reflects a didactic purpose. She is a model for change suggested to an audience that is likely to include many young people who consider themselves Mexican Americans.

The teachers are portrayed as unidimensional figures whose identity is hidden behind a cruel white mask. This dramatic recourse, already introduced in the characterization of the rancher in *Las dos caras*, allows the playwright to maintain unity throughout the classroom scenes as the teachers remain distant and predictable while the focus of interest is on the interaction among the students.[16] The *acto* ends as students from the audience converge on the stage to solicit entrance into institutions of higher learning, a dramatic strategy that coincided with the movement for the establishment of Chicano studies in many colleges throughout the southwestern United States. The influence of Teatro Campesino during this time became evident as thousands of Chicano students organized in a concerted effort to obtain educational reforms. At this juncture the Teatro reached its greatest success in linking theater with social mobilization, a telling indication of the power of art.

Transitional *Actos*

As mentioned before, the criticism Valdez has toward attitudes that relegate Chicanos to a marginal historical dimension is twofold. On the one hand, he seeks to denounce a number of injustices exerted from outside the Chicano community. On the other hand, he appeals to an in-group normative model to censure any self-defeating type of behavior. Such a double-edged satirical purpose is evident in *The Militants*. This brief *acto* portrays two intense but naive Chicano activists who, in spite of their vitriolic denunciation of the academic system, kill each other after an absurd ideological competition. Behind their self-destruction stands the figure of a perverse Anglo-American university administrator, Dr. Bolillo, plotting and rejoicing at the extremists' empty rhetoric. The seminal idea for this *acto* had appeared in *No sacó nada* in a scene where Monty mimics the slogans of radical nationalists in order to impress Florence, his Anglo-American girlfriend. In *The Militants*, however, the targets of satire are Chicano students who mindlessly paraphrase political slogans:

> What is that pair of something every macho has in the barrio? That makes every revolutionary willing to die at any moment? Like me, I'm

willing to die! Any pigs in the audience? Kill me! Go on, I'm ready! KILL
ME! I'm not afraid, because I know what it takes: a pair of . . . BIGOTES
[mustaches]. Viva la Huelga! Viva la Causa! Viva la Raza! Viva la Revolución! Viva los bigotes!! (*Actos* 97–98)

This brief *acto* is notable because Valdez, who had introduced
characters rebelling against the dominant culture, now criticizes
students who foolishly adopt such a role. Chicano militancy is now
presented as an empty formula, and the role played by the two student radicals resembles that of a boastful soldier *(miles gloriosus)*
whose bravado is but a hollow epic gesture. In *The Militants* the
message is that divisiveness is the result of false consciousness,
whereas the positive norm is represented by a return to sober social
activism. In his introductory essay to the *Actos*, the playwright
gives a warning concerning the limits of the figurative language used
by the activists.

It is particularly important for teatro Chicano to draw a distinction between what is theater and what is reality. A demonstration with a thousand Chicanos, all carrying flags and picket signs, shouting CHICANO
POWER! is not the revolution. It is theater about the revolution. The
people must act in *reality* not on stage (which could be anywhere, even
a sidewalk) in order to achieve real change. (*Actos* 2)

In 1970 Valdez directed two *actos* that focused again on the plight
of the farmworkers and their efforts to improve working conditions
in the fields. In *Vietnam campesino* he dramatizes these sociopolitical issues in terms that may appeal to the young urban audiences
the Teatro has cultivated. It depicts the political role of powerful
agricultural interests who support the military establishment while
receiving their subsidies and who have launched a concerted effort
against Chicano *campesinos* [farmworkers] and Vietnamese farmworkers:

[GENERAL] (POINTS AT VIETNAMESE) Farmworkers just like them farmworkers. (POINTS AT CAMPESINOS, THEN BACK AT VIETNAMESE) Campesinos just like them campesinos. (POINTS AGAIN) Poor people just like
them poor people. (POINTS AGAIN) And we've been killing them for ten
years. (*Actos* 119)

In blending these two themes, agriculture and war, Valdez points out
to both rural and urban Chicanos that their lives are intimately de-
pendent on international events. This thematic duality also marked
a most significant transition for the Teatro Campesino at a time
when it ceased to address rural concerns and began to articulate issues of interest to urban audiences.

The second of these plays, *Huelguistas,* is a brief and plotless vignette that depicts various farmworkers confronting a ranchowner (Patroncito) and his hired *contratista* (Coyote). The primary purpose of *Huelguistas* is no longer to convince workers to abandon the fields and join the strikers, but to provide a background or motif in what is basically a musical dramatization. At this point in his career, Luis Valdez had expanded his public to include national and international audiences, conditions that allowed him to experiment with new facets in the Teatro's repertoire and permitted him to bring to the foreground the entertainment aspects of the performances. In *Huelguistas* music assumes a central function. An important factor in this musical emphasis involves lessening the importance of culture and language: the company now required plays that could be presented to non-Chicano audiences at home and abroad. Indeed, European, Anglo-American, and Latin American monolingual audiences would find difficulty in understanding detailed references to Chicano life, colloquialisms, or the code switches frequently employed in the *Actos.*[17]

Soldado razo

The final phase of this early, Teatro Campesino, period in Valdez' career is represented by *Soldado razo,* a study on the effect of the Vietnam War on a Chicano family.[18] In comparison with previous *actos, Soldado razo* realistically projects characters with psychological depth. The focus is on the motivations and emotional responses of the victims of war. In this denunciation of the culture of war, therefore, the portrayal of human caricatures is no longer viable. Although oppression still looms in the background, Valdez illustrates how personal decisions—sometimes apparently inconsequential choices—may result in great suffering.

The *acto* shows the protagonist, Johnny, and his immediate family circle formed by his father, mother, younger brother, and fiancée. This is a typical Chicano family with positive aspects as well as shortcomings, and the audience can not fail to sympathize with their predictable attitudes—whether it be the false bravado of the father, who has had a few beers to hide his pride at seeing his son reach adulthood; the mother's calm resignation at the departure of her son; or the brother's youthful energy that disrupts the decorum at the dinner table. An important theme here is Johnny's rite of passage into adulthood, represented by his engagement and his leaving to fight in the war. Since we know from the beginning the fatal outcome that awaits Johnny, the events before his departure acquire added significance. Irony intensifies the pathos of Johnny's family, whose love and good intentions actually guide him to his death.

The tragedy of Johnny's family lies in their helplessness to avert his death: an inescapable fate that is sealed by their acceptance of the ideology of war. This message is dramatized by the figure of the Death narrator—a refinement of the masked figures of early *actos*—who serves as a perverse quasi-director, conducting and interpreting events that are only perceived by the public, while Johnny, his family, and his girlfriend remain unaware of the larger social forces that help shape their destinies. As in other *actos* performed by Teatro Campesino, the playwright's criticism is directed toward ideas and practices that threaten Chicanos, whether in the internalization of values that confine them to playing the roles of victims or that arise directly from the centers of power in U.S. society.

The Death narrator tells the story of Johnny, shown at first at home as he prepares to leave for Vietnam and, later, at the frontlines as he writes home of the horrors he has witnessed and urges other Chicanos not to enlist in the armed forces. This double perspective of Johnny at home and at war establishes the correlation between the human dimension of Chicanos and the innocent people of Vietnam who suffer the ravages of war. In its role as narrator, Death at first provides humorous insights into the events depicted but gradually recedes into the background, until it finally appears, as a deus ex machina, mechanistically describing Johnny's fate. Personal responsibility serves as a thread throughout the *acto*, linking the psychological makeup of the characters portrayed. This approach helps demonstrate how family life, community expectations, and historical context are closely interwoven in determining the behavior of the characters. That is, Valdez makes Johnny and his family directly involved in the decision to prolong the war, although a fine balance is maintained between their personal acquiescence in his participation and the societal forces that organize their experience.

The criticism of community values in *Soldado razo* serves a purpose already evident throughout the *actos:* in combating the ills that affect Chicanos, it is necessary to condemn practices that are self-defeating. This self-reflexive condemnation, however, does not mean a total rejection of the Chicano community. Indeed, what renders *Soldado razo* a touching piece is Valdez' intimate dramatization of Chicano family life: the *acto* is an ironic depiction of family foibles that, nevertheless, recognizes the underlying emotional strength the family provides its members. Thus, in portraying their psychological depth, Valdez supersedes the conception of Chicanos as merely "types," a view that he had satirized in *Los vendidos*. This dramatic shift signals a move away from satire and toward a generic borderline where Chicano life may be conveyed in predominantly tragic or comic terms.

The *mito*

In a relatively short time—1965 to 1971—the *actos* were performed and imitated by dozens of Chicano community theatrical groups throughout the country.[19] During this period Teatro Campesino was awarded numerous prizes and achieved its international reputation. Yet always searching for new dramatic possibilities, Valdez explored another genre: the *mito*, a religious performance that allegorizes figures and motifs from pre-Columbian mythologies (Shank 61–67). Interest in religious themes was not new for Valdez, whose first play, *The Theft*, written in 1959, satirized contemporary mores and underscored the lack of Christian charity.[20] This focus on religion had appeared before, too, in the puppet show *La conquista de México*, a parody of the Spanish conquest and the domination of the native American cultures. In contrast to the clear satirical purpose of the *actos*, the *mito* represented a significant generic change that conveyed a contrasting perspective on Chicano life. In his poem "Pensamiento serpentino," Valdez outlines this new ideological thrust which may be summarized as follows:

1. Due to their colonized status, Chicanos have lost a vision of their own condition.
2. In order to supersede their immediate negative situation, Chicanos must become neo-Mayans and adopt the wisdom of ancient pre-Columbian culture.
3. Cosmic man attains a superior view of mankind, an ideal level that is beyond the immediate historical circumstances of a particular group identity.

In this new orientation, the individual, disregarding the authority of norms, must operate from a value-free perspective. Since topical references are inherent to satire, Valdez' new vision is beyond this possibility:

Para el hombre cósmico	[For cosmic man
EL CAN de los Mayas antiguos	THE CAN of the old Mayans
la muerte no existe	death does not exist
Racial distinctions	
no existen	do not exist
límites materiales	material limitations

no existen   do not exist
nations, wealth, fashions,
hatreds, envidias, greed,   envy
the lust for power
no existen,   do not exist.]

not even the lust for
CHICANO POWER (9–10)

Yet, Valdez advocates change as an inescapable process:

But REALITY es una Gran Serpiente
a great serpent
that moves and changes
and keeps crawling
out of its dead skin
. . . .
And so
los oprimidos del mundo   [the oppressed of the world
continue to become
los liberadores   the liberators
in the true progress of cosas   things
and the Chicano is part of the
process
el proceso cósmico that will   the cosmic process]
LIBERATE OUR CONQUISTADORES
or their descendants. (2–3)

Implicit in this new approach to Chicano culture is the suggestion that the satirical attacks underlying the *actos* can be superseded by a spiritual humanism. Accordingly, a new morality is offered in the Mayan concept "IN LAK 'ECH: *Tú eres mi otro yo*" (You are my other self) that provides a pre-Columbian equivalent of the Christian "Love thy neighbor as thyself." From this perspective of a new vision, Valdez declared: "But above all / to be CHICANO is to LOVE GOD."[21]

Beyond the Teatro Campesino

If satire is a genre that conveys an opponent in terms of marginal qualities—while urging the adoption of the satirist's own norm as superior—Valdez' introduction of the *mito* and the musical drama were generic shifts that had important implications for his employment of satire. Since the *mito*'s central orientation is the affirmation of pre-Columbian virtues and a heroic legacy, its dignified and prophetic qualities belie any alternative human rivalry and thus eliminate the need to launch a satiric attack. Similarly, the entertainment qualities of predominantly musical dramatizations dispel the urgency for change that is characteristic of satire.

Another important artistic change occurred when the Teatro Campesino purchased land and moved to San Juan Bautista, California, in 1974. The financial, logistic, and theatrical demands imposed by this move led Valdez to expand his own area of activity independently of Teatro Campesino. Thus, in 1978 Valdez opened a play in Los Angeles, *Zoot Suit*, whose success ushered him into a new career in commercial theater and film. The narrative structure of *Zoot Suit* has numerous parallels to the *actos*, including its denunciation of the grave injustice committed to a group of *pachucos* during World War II. A central focus of the play, however, is on the psychological conflict that confronts the protagonist, Henry Reyna, a tragic figure who agonizes over the limited options he encounters during a period marked by profound social inequity. *Zoot Suit* maintains a number of dramatic similarities with *Soldado razo*, including the themes of war, family, and love, as well as its realistic depiction of individual character and the presence of an omniscient narrator (the Pachuco). As in *Soldado razo*, *Zoot Suit* has displaced the satirical pungency of the earlier *actos*; in the play (later made into a film), music plays a predominant function.

In a most interesting generic development, the play *"I Don't Have to Show You No Stinking Badges"* (1986) translates the comic figures of the *actos* into theatrical comedy that parodies the television sit-com. This re-creation includes the portrayal of Chicanos as professional actors who are assigned irrelevant, stereotypical roles in Hollywood films. It also involves substituting the profanity in the *actos* for the humor appropriate to American television. Perhaps the most significant change in the play is the thematic shift away from barrio struggles to the representation of the anguish that confronts Chicano middle-class characters—a nuclear family consisting of a couple of professional actors and their college-educated son. But most notable in *Badges* is the absence of culprit figures as fair subjects of satirical attack—presumably a group of "media *patroncitos*" bent on denying professional Chicano artists the opportunity to act in serious roles—in what is inherently a comedy with tragic overtones.

Music had always been an important element in the representations of the Teatro. In *Huelguistas* Valdez had experimented with a musical dramatization of an *acto* that included portrayals of the Patroncito and Don Coyote. Similarly, in *Zoot Suit* the musical aspect of the performance becomes central to the play. This new generic development is further explored in the theatrical, television, and video productions of *Corridos*, a reinterpretation of Mexican traditional ballads *(corridos)*, as well as in the film *La Bamba*, the biography of rock star Richie Valens (Ricardo Valenzuela).

Any comparison between the *actos* of Teatro Campesino and Valdez' later work for television, film, and theater is likely to be uneven, since the constraints, possibilities, and audiences of one media are totally different from the other. Satire thrives, indeed cannot exist, without bitter conflict: the cause of striking farmworkers or the protests of students represented excellent opportunities for its employment. The mass media and public later addressed by Valdez posed special requirements unimaginable in the early years of Teatro Campesino—especially the need to address the normative values of a sizable, mainstream, Anglo-American audience.[22] This public would not be particularly favorable toward supporting representations that involve controversial and highly politicized interethnic issues. Thus, it may not be surprising if the most popular (and profitable) productions are those in which social criticism is least evident, unlike the *actos* where the skill in attacking the satiric target is a primary criterion in assessing the success of a performance.[23] Yet there is a danger in the employment of Chicano images in comedy, without the benefit of satire, since this may be interpreted as a reaffirmation of the dominant norm and a return to the representation of Chicanos in stereotypical terms, a problem that Valdez had masterfully addressed in *Los vendidos*.

The figures that Valdez created for Teatro Campesino exist within an imaginary continuum that extends from one extreme of power and wealth to another of defenselessness and poverty. These two poles are clearly defined along cultural and racial lines, one Anglo-American and white, the other Chicano and dark. The anti-Chicano characters, who illustrate the abuses perpetrated on the marginal, are generally satirized figures who portray social and psychological maladies: ranch owners whose single-minded materialism generates economic inequality, socially myopic teachers who distort learning experiences, institutional officials who govern with cultural and racial insensitivity, and unscrupulous politicians who misuse taxpayers' money. These characters, following the Theophrastian tradition, depict types, rather than three-dimensional individuals. The audience must then assess the truth of the satiric attack posed by these figures and interpret their significance in relation to daily experience. This link between fiction and reality has a doubly important function: a series of comical figures entertain the public, but the values inherent in their imaginary behavior are of immediate and vital importance to the audience.

With an apparent artlessness, the characters in the Teatro Campesino are exaggerated, and plots and dialogues are blatantly contrived. This overemphasis, to the point of distortion, is a parody of theatrical conventions in what must be understood as a satire on form. Stylistic devices thus provide an iconoclastic atmosphere where all normative values are automatically ridiculed. It is an earthy and festive tendency evident in the humorous use of scatological references, maledictions, and sexual allusions. In this sense the *actos* observe the function Mikhail Bakhtin ascribed to the marketplace in his study of Rabelais: "[It is] the center of all that is unofficial; it enjoyed a certain extraterritoriality in a world of official ideology, it always remained 'with the people' " (153–154). Valdez noted a corresponding attitude on the part of the audience was required for Chicano theater: "Without the palomía [crowd] there, laughing, crying and sharing whatever is on stage, the teatros will dry up and die. If the Raza will not come to the theater, then the theater must go to the Raza" (*Actos* 4).

The dramatization of long-felt social dissatisfaction within the community helped establish a rapport between Teatro Campesino and Chicano audiences. The themes, as well as the tone, of the Teatro responded to a number of contemporary issues, such as the Civil Rights Movement and the Vietnam War. These two events, which profoundly altered the American consciousness, helped bring to the forefront issues of racial, economic, and social redress. Valdez was an effective voice in linking these concerns to his attack on attitudes that had confined Chicanos to marginality, a situation the *actos* of Teatro Campesino denounced as dehumanizing. These historical conditions encouraged the emergence of a new generation of Chicano scholars, professionals, and activists who proceeded to question the conditions that had molded their communities. In this sense the art of Valdez was decisive in molding the cultural consciousness of his generation.

3. José Montoya: From the RCAF to the Trio Casindio

José Montoya was born in New Mexico, where he spent the first ten years of his life. In the early 1940s, his family moved to California, where they worked on farms along the rural and semiurban landscape of the San Joaquin Valley. Montoya's career as an artist began upon his return from serving a tour of duty in the U.S. Navy. He enrolled at a junior college in San Diego, then transferred to a prestigious art college in Oakland, and later received a master's degree in fine arts. Those years in the San Francisco Bay Area, in the late 1950s and early 1960s, were of critical importance in his intellectual and artistic development. He was a close witness to the emergence of the American "counterculture," that formative period that generated the diverse "movements" known as beat, Free Speech, hippie, and antiwar. These experiences led Montoya to forge a Chicano aesthetic in which marginal figures struggle heroically to overcome insurmountable barriers that threaten their predominantly humanistic values.[1]

In an important stage of his literary apprenticeship, Montoya rejected the conventional representations of Mexicans in American literature. He objected to such books as Steinbeck's *Tortilla Flat*, where Mexicans are portrayed as lazy and lustful characters "making love in the mud." Such scenes were unimaginable to someone familiar with the strict conventional mores observed within the Chicano community. The novice writer also noted that literary texts that included foreign words or phrases were readily accepted by his teachers, yet strident objections were raised about his own work because it included Chicano colloquialisms or code switches between English and Spanish. These and numerous other experiences caused him to question the attitudes toward Chicanos that confined them to negative, stereotypical images.

The productive period in Montoya's writing career began in the early 1960s, after he left Oakland and became a high school art teacher at a small community in northern California. The success of César Chávez in organizing the farmworkers' strike at Delano had a profound effect on Montoya, who, as had other Chicanos at that time, initiated a personal reevaluation of American life. Sympathizing with the cause of the striking farmworkers, Montoya participated in the historic march from Delano to Sacramento in 1965. By this time he had begun writing poems in which he spoke of his experiences as a child and an adolescent farmworker. Some of his best-known poetic pieces were written during this period: his collection in *El sol y los de abajo*, "La jefita" (Valdez, *Aztlán* 266–268), and "El Louie" (Valdez, *Aztlán* 333–337). When in 1969 the Berkeley journal *El Grito* published some of his work, Montoya had already begun reading his poetry at public forums. These readings have continued throughout the years and have made him a well-known figure to audiences of Chicano literature at national and international forums.[2] Although his merit rests on his few published poems, he is regarded as a prominent Chicano writer. The body of Montoya's work, however, either remains unpublished or is available only in editions of limited circulation. As a consequence, the corpus of his work has yet to receive the critical attention it deserves.[3]

Comic and Satiric Figures

Throughout his poetic corpus, Montoya portrays figures that may be considered marginal. Because the poet seeks to depict these figures positively, he employs utmost caution to avoid the reinforcing of stereotypes. He solves this problem by adopting an in-group perspective that provides an implicit rejection of those norms imposed externally and which have customarily served to judge Chicanos in negative terms. Thus, in Montoya's world a character's self-realization inevitably comes into conflict with the normative values of American mainstream society. The rhetorical techniques that Montoya employs are not always readily apparent: a comic veneer may chastise a transgressor, but there is a tacit defense of Chicano life in a pointed satirical attack against its detractors. His poetic world, therefore, represents an affirmation of the values of the dispossessed and an implicit condemnation of those oppressive forces that deny Chicanos the possibility of living a humanized existence.

Although Montoya's humor is closely aligned to Mexican culture, his thematic choices respond to the marginal status of Chicanos in American society. This is evident in the attitude of self-deprecation he adopts in "Moco Pome" (*El sol* 42), where the narrative voice appeals to peer solidarity. In this brief poem, Montoya portrays him-

self in ridiculous terms in order to remind the reader of their mutual
obligations that bind them in honesty and brotherly concern:

And if you see
a moco on my   [a mucus on my
Bigote—   mustache—]

Don't suffer
My shame and
Don't punish
Me with silence . . .

Tell me about it!

A related traditional comic convention is that of an insignificant
character given an incongruously grandiose role. In Spanish literature this figure appears most clearly in nonsense popular speech
where epic features are often ascribed to insignificant individuals,
or animals, with predictable humorous results.[4] In "Metamorphosis—or Guilty with an Explanation" (*In Formation* 22), the poet
ironically depicts himself as he is released from the police station:

I walked to
The street unescorted
Y me fui por toda   [And I went along
La Efe and it was   F Street]
Raining hard and I

Began to whistle
  And I was the
  cucaracha that   [cockroach]
  got away from
  the raid of the
  Black Flag—

Todo catiado, con   [All beat up, with
Una antena caida   one fallen antenna]
My cockroach integrity
Intact!

A similarly mocking depiction is evident in the song "Rocinante"
(*Casindio*), where the poet's car bears the name of Quijote's horse
and, as its cognomen, also is ascribed masculine characteristics.[5]
Montoya's Rocinante, like its Cervantean predecessor becomes involved with a member of the opposite sex:

En un viaje pa' Coachella
Una troquita se encontró
Y por andar puchando troca
El mofle se le cayó.

[On a trip to Coachella
he met a little (female) truck
and while pushing the truck
lost his muffler.]

Here the incongruity between the vehicle's sexual aggressiveness
and its actual ridiculous performance underlies this comic encounter between the poet's old but faithful car and the presumedly attractive *troquita* [little female truck].

Montoya's poetry includes a number of other figures also derived
from the traditional comic and satiric conventions of the Western
canon. Thus, drawing from the practice of ridiculing physical dis-
abilities, he alludes to the sister of one of his young peers, callously
nicknamed *la coja* (the lame one) (*El sol* 1). Similarly, a handicap is
mentioned in referring to a hunchbacked woman said to be a witch:
"La curandera, bruja, life-giving / Jorobada," a figure that provokes
the laughter of the children (*El sol* 36).

Montoya feels great affinity for the indigenous cultures of the
Americas. This admiration led to the creation of a series of figures
based on the concept of Chicanos as *Casindio* (almost Indian). The
name originates in a story in which two figures, the Derelict Dog
and Don Chepo, tell the latter's grandson that Chicanos are almost
Indian:

> "All Chicano tribes belong to the Casindio Nation."
> "That makes all Chicanos Casindios!" adds the Derelict Dog.
> "Why?" the boy asks.
> "Porque somos casi indios" [Because we are almost Indians], le res-
> ponde [responds] patiently el abuelo [grandfather]. Both oldtimers want
> to laugh, but they realize that the boy still has not gotten it. So, they
> explain again, in more simple terms, how there are several Chicano
> tribes that make up the Casindio Nation. And because his pal's father is
> a Chicano Sun Dancer, he belongs to the *Yamero* tribe. "The *Yameros*
> are the Chicano tribe closest to the *Masindio*, the original Native
> American," sez don Chepo.

There are many other imaginary tribes in the *Casindio* nation: the
Yaquisieran, the *Yafumaron,* the *Yapaqués,* the *Nochoises.* All of
these parody the sound of tribal names but have an actual meaning
either in Spanish or in English. Thus, the *Yamero* are "almost
there"; the *Masindio* are "more Indian"; the "*Yaquisieran*" are
"those who wished they were"; the *Yafumaron*—being marijuana
smokers—"have already smoked"; the *Yapaqués*—who hate to be
called Chicanos—may be disregarded as "what's the use" [¿ya para
qué?]; and the *Nochoises,* a name that is evident in English, are said
to be, ironically, Plains Indians. The Chicanos belonging to these

fictional tribes, however, are false Indians, and their comic names
are an implicit reference to their cultural inadequacies. A further
elaboration of these linguistic parodies is found in a relatively recent
poem in which the words "should" and "could" are used: "The Xura
Cura Tribe Reports" (*In Formation* n.p.), in which Montoya recounts a trip to Europe made by a group of Chicanos. After failing
to establish rapport with their European hosts, some Chicano scholars acted unkindly toward their own peers. Montoya is critical of
such behavior and laments his own helplessness in articulating a
forceful Chicano position.

> Perhaps that explains why
> The should-a could-a
> could-a should-a blues
> Have settled in—
> I should a done this
> done that!
> Could have—no excuse
> Should make effort to say
> About what I did do,
> Could!

In Montoya's poetry there is a pervasive spiritual undercurrent:
some of the religious figures he portrays are serious; others are employed for comic or satiric purposes. The conventional humorous
figure of the sinner, for example, frequently appears in relation to
the observance of Roman Catholic ritual. In "Misa en Fowler" (*El
sol* 8), young boys ridicule the seriousness of the faithful who are
praying at church. Such depictions are generally presented good-
humoredly, as in the scene with the older people at church in the
poem "Es que se va morir don Chema" (Because Don Chema is going
to die) (*El sol* 18):

> All the viejitos en   [old people
> Voz alta determined to   Loud voice
>   Gain absolution for all
>   those sweet sins of the past . . .
> ME ARREPIENTO, DIOS MIO   I REPENT, MY GOD
> CON UN SUSPIRO Y UNA SONRISA . . .   WITH A SIGH AND SMILE]

The poet's satiric vein becomes evident in "Irish Priest and Chicano Sinners" (*El sol* 16) where the church's imposition of European
priests is decried as serving to alienate the faithful in the Chicano
community. The latter never "saw a real priest," that is, those that
would be culturally sensitive to Chicano congregations. Instead, the
believer is restricted to the services of priests from Spain or Ireland;

it is an obvious criticism toward the negative status that the U.S. Roman Catholic church accords the Chicano community.[6] These foreign spiritual leaders, devoid of the understanding of Chicano culture, were "full of bitterness" toward assignments in locations they must have considered as demeaning posts. For their part the Chicano believers only perceived alien priests who condemned "all those sinning Mexicans!" And since the European priests were fair and blond—just as the rich in town—the only inference that could be drawn was the inherent evil of being poor, dark, and Mexican.

So bad he was finally sent to
Hell by Spaniards and Irishmen,

And nobody bothered to explain
Any of it to him.

Social and religious alienation may produce an ambivalent system of social values. Thus, in the poem "Jack off Hangover" (*El sol* 13), the culprit of masturbation confronts his realization that the feminine holy figures at church remind him of his mother and sisters. This is a rare insight into Chicano male adolescence. The boy protagonist is tormented by the possibility that his sexual fantasies may contaminate the boundaries established by religious principle and social taboo. Attempting to dispel the possible sinfulness or immorality involved in this conception of the sexuality of female kin or feminine deities, he struggles against the thought by recalling figures from popular culture—such as Lois Lane and Wonder Woman— or from outside the group—an Anglo girl, Maggie Griggs. The latter are counterpoised ironically, since their roles serve to alleviate his imaginary guilt by appealing to his desire for "permissible" feminine figures.

Adolescent desire is also portrayed in "Early Pieces" (*El sol* 1), a comic portrayal of male children as they perform a ritual that involves claims of exaggerated sexual prowess. The first-person narrative voice describes how three curious boys enter a bar and pretend to shine shoes while actually they intend to observe the new barmaid. At first they are "embarrassed at each other," but upon perceiving her lifting her dress "a little" become "all escamaus [frightened] and confused" and run out. Yet when the boys relate this experience to their peers, it is selectively re-created as they start bragging "how we got it from the wetback cantinera." That the "adventure" is a failure from beginning to end renders the boys as comic figures unable to maintain an ideal of masculinity. But implicit in such humorous depiction is an ironic commentary on the overwhelming demands faced by adolescent males. The title "Early Pieces" intensifies this irony, suggesting that the practice of exaggerating sexual performance continues into adulthood but that such "epic triumphs" are substantially the product of male imagination.

The assimilated Chicano is represented, negatively, as an awkward extension of Anglo-American life. The protagonist in the poem "Jesse" (*El sol* 7), for example, is a young rural Chicano who struggles to succeed in school as an athlete. While sports has been one of the few open avenues into academia for minority students, Montoya's criticism is directed toward such efforts when they involve the internalization of self-defeating values. In his ironic description of this figure, Montoya avoids a melodramatic tone, given the ethnic origin of "Jesse" (Jesús)—hence the reference to the biblical "valley of tears"—while satirizing the arrogance that Jesse will display once his education provides him with knowledge and a middle-class status:

Forget Jess[e] en el valle de lagrimitas
With a capital "L" and jest let Jess[e]
HAVE AND KNOW.

Somewhat disdainfully Montoya portrays Jesse as wearing a "beret patch" over his varsity letter, a commentary on the incongruence of being part of the Chicano movement while attempting to maintain a status as an athlete at school.[7] Jesse's efforts are those of a foolish figure:

Run your heart out boy con brilliantine in
Your greaser hair for scholarships and a hot dog
                                    white.

In spite of his efforts to gain glory for his coach and an alma (mater) that is "momless," Jess is condemned to racial marginality: "BUT JEZ DON'T MARRY MAH DOUDER, HEAH????"

In the song "Lulac Cadillac" (*Casindio*), Montoya satirizes the opportunism of Chicano middle-class administrators.[8] In Montoya's poem a member of this group is shown as a pretentious figure—he now drives a Cadillac—who owes his recent affluence to the political paternalism that token minorities receive in Washington, D.C. Upon his return to the community, he adopts a different wardrobe and has a new woman companion who seems as pretentious as he is:

It's been a while
Que no te vía

Con esos trapos y esa ruca
No te conocía

[It's been a while
since I have seen you
with those rags and old lady
I didn't recognize you.]

The poetic voice reminds the deviant Chicano of his group membership and of the injustices still prevalent toward the Chicano community: "Just don't forget / How it's supposed to be." By employing English colloquialisms, it alludes ironically to the loss of culture:

You're gonna lose
It seems to me
Your chile eatin'
Ability

In "The Movement Has Gone for Its Ph.D. over at the University—Or the Gang Wars Are Back" (*In Formation* 35–37), Montoya ridicules those Chicanos who as student radicals criticized the institutions they have now come to serve. Their present indifference toward their Chicano communities contrasts sharply with their former adoption of revolutionary stances:

Where do you suppose they've gone,
All those bad-assed bigotones
Que llegaron shouting RAZA
Y VIVA EL BARRIO
And they couldn't even roll their Rs?

In attacking their middle-class values, the poet portrays them as opportunists whose true commitment has been to their own material gain. It is an implicit condemnation of their intellectual irresponsibility whereby the fulfillment of a Chicano agenda has been subverted for the advancement of an elite:

Y los profes y estudiantes siguen

Siempre diligentemente pa'delante

All keep searching for those stipends
in the sky.

[And the teachers and students
continue
Always diligently advancing
forward]

A similar attitude is evident in "Los They Are Us," (*In Formation* 58–59), where the poet decries the existence of Chicanos who hold positions of authority but lack any concern for the betterment of their communities. He compares the attitude of Anglo-Americans who are callous toward Chicano communities—"los they" (them)—with those Chicano figures who imitate them blindly: "Only the system remains the same, / But the faces are *our* faces!" "Los they" appear under different disguises:

policemen:
>   Today they beat up lowriders like
>   They beat up Pachucos before

teachers:
>   Antes los they used to put us in   [before
>   M.R. classes—today they do it in   mentally retarded]
>   Two languages

lawyers:
>   Before los public defenders nos
>   Mandaban al tabique and today, once   [sent us to jail]
>   MECHA militants are sending us up
>   and charging us for it.

or politicians:
>   Y los políticos used us as they
>   Broke bread with our leaders,
>   And they lied to us like politicians
>   Lie, and today the lies are the
>   Same as we break pan dulce and have   [sweet bread
>   Canela clatches—   cinnamon]

The figure of the deviant in Montoya's poetry is assessed according to community values. Because norms imposed by external and unsympathetic standards are often broken by Chicanos, the transgressors are seen favorably or compassionately. This situation requires that the judge of behavior be cognizant of the relationship the Chicano community has with the surrounding society. Thus, rather than belittling truancy, juvenile delinquency, and poverty, the poetic voice places emphasis on the negative role played by diverse representatives of American institutions. The image of Anglo strangers invading the sacredness of a Chicano community is especially poignant in "El sol y los de abajo" (*El sol* 38) where the tranquillity of the poet's family is disrupted by an alien presence:

>   Cuando no era el probation officer   [when it wasn't the
>   Era el councilor de la escuela,   [It was the school's counselor
>   La jura or some long haired,   [The police]
>   Lostlamb, maveric chick offering
>   Us the world so she could write
>   Her thesis.

Instead of American culture as a bastion of reason, freedom, and prosperity, in "Don't Ever Lose Your Driver's License" (*In Formation*

46) the poet skeptically observes the road from a Greyhound Bus that is transporting old and poor people:

> And the dreams seem nearer
> As huge, smiling billboards
> Proclaim a grand America
> Out there—somewhere—.

In his poem "Always Do What You Are Told the Best Way You Know How" (*In Formation* 45), the poetic voice portrays scorn for authority while being forced to demonstrate respect for court proceedings:

> The bailiff gave me
> One of those
> You're-on-my-turf-now-punk
> Looks and exhorted me to
> Call the judge YOUR HONOR
>
> So I said *fuck you very much*
>
> What!
>
> I said *"Thank you very much,*
> Your Honor!"
>
> Oh, I see. That's better.
>
> Uh, hum
> Dije yo . . .   [I said . . .]

This attitude of distrust toward the symbols of American respectability is also evident in the poem "Pobre Viejo Walt Whitman" (Poor old man Walt Whitman) (*In Formation* 3). Montoya satirizes the figure of Whitman as a singer of the epic of American democracy and his prophetic voice is cast as false:

> When the good gray poet
> Imposed his virile image
> Upon the impotent people no
> Envisionó en su locura   [Did not envision in his madness
> Stooped-shouldered junkies
> Aching to get straight and
> Hip-swinging he-men
> Abrazándose en callejones oscuros.   Hugging in dark alleys].

In his song "Marinero mariguano" (Pot-smoking sailor) (Personal recording), Montoya portrays himself as a sailor during the Korean War, providing a comic view of the U.S. Navy. The epic role of sailors is seen from the perspective of a nonconformist who participates in the war on his own terms. He breaks the established civilian and wartime codes, having been arrested previously on charges of possessing marijuana. After spending some time in jail, he is transferred to a minesweeper where he meets others who share his unconventional life-style:

En el barco me encontré
al Beto del Paso, Texas
me ofreció la bienvenida
y unos toques de su tecla
me dice:—Aquí no hay fijón
aquí la tenemos hecha.—

[In the boat I met
Beto from El Paso, Texas
He welcomed me
and offered me some puffs from his joint
and tells me: "It's cool here, we got it made here."]

The narrative voice mockingly laments the lack of discipline among the crew: the captain drinks and plays cards with the sailors, and the inexperienced officers are afraid of the sea. When the captain's drinking causes the minesweeper to sink, the poet and other sailors are saved only because they are busy smoking marijuana: "por estar rolando un leño / no oímos ni la explosión" (while rolling a joint / we didn't hear the explosion). The narrative voice summarizes his experiences at war by warning other Chicanos against enlisting. He questions the value of being awarded medals as long as Chicanos are kept in a lower social status:

Ya no se anden enlistando
le digo yo a mis carnales
de qué sirven las medallas
si nos ven como animales,
ahí les dejo sus bisteckes
yo prefiero mis nopales.

[Don't enlist anymore
I urge my brothers
what's the use of medals
if they see us as animals
You can have your steaks
I prefer my *nopales* (cactus).]

Montoya's position on the participation of Chicanos in U.S. wars is not limited to the denunciation of the abuses or shortcomings of superiors. Such a comic portrayal is already common in U.S. popular culture; going further, Montoya attacks the very basis of armed conflicts and especially the inappropriate involvement of Chicanos:

Yo nunca he tenido pleito
con los coreanos del norte
pero el gringo entremetido
se mete aunque no le . . . importe,
y ahí voy yo como tarugo,
es tiempo que me las corte.

[I have never had trouble
with the North Koreans
but the nosy gringo
gets involved . . . anyhow
and there I go, like a fool
It's time for me to quit.]

The satire on Chicano presence in U.S. armed conflicts is also launched from a nationalistic perspective. Accordingly, Chicano soldiers should fight for their own cause, under their own flag:

Ya con esta me despido
con respeto al ancho mar,
no pierdo las esperanzas
de volverlo a navegar,
pero en un buque chicano
con la bandera de Aztlán.

[I bid you farewell
with respect for the wide seas
I don't lose my hope
to sail them again
but on a Chicano boat
carrying the flag of Aztlán.]

A similar political approach is evident in the poem "Pesadilla Yanqui" (*Casindio*) where the attack is directed toward U.S. Intervention in Central America. Writing within the tradition of the genre known as *canción de protesta* (protest song), the poet establishes his solidarity with the Latin American people and denounces the United States as an enemy of their freedom:

Desde las tierras meshicas
Hasta la punta de Chile
. . . .
Llevamos el mismo sueño
de encontrar la libertad.

[From the Meshica (Mexican) lands
To the tip of Chile
. . . .
We carry the same dream
Of finding freedom.]

Thus, the other side of the Yankee nightmare (intervention) is a call
to awaken to the reality of a united and free Latin America:

> Porque hay una pesadilla
> Que nos roba la unidad
> Y de ese mal sueño yankee
> Es tiempo de despertar.

> [There is a nightmare
> That robs us of unity
> And from that bad Yankee dream
> It's time to awaken.]

Montoya's Satiric Discourse: *El sol y los de abajo*

Code switching is common among bilinguals. This phenomenon
consists in alternation between two languages, both between and
within sentences. In spite of its apparent randomness, however,
most linguists believe this practice is governed by rules, although
there is yet to be a consensus as to the nature of the rules employed
by code switchers.[9] Both extralinguistic and linguistic factors have
been adduced to explain the alternation from one language to another. In a study of Norwegian dialectal switches, for example, Jan
Peter Blom and John Gumperz concluded that selection of linguistic
alternates was both patterned and predictable on the basis of certain
features of the local social system. That is, the use of local dialect
reflected local experiences while standard Norwegian was employed
on topics with a Pan-Norwegian orientation. In another study of
Puerto Rican bilinguals, Shana Poplack inferred "that the code
switching mode proceeds from that area of the bilingual's grammar
where the surface structures of L1 and L2 [i.e., languages 1 and 2]
overlap, and code switching, rather than representing debasement of
linguistic skill, is actually a sensitive indicator of bilingual ability."

In addition to these strictly social functions, code switching may
be used artistically. The bilingual expressiveness in José Montoya's
poetry illustrates how code switching—in the manner that is customarily found among many Chicano bilinguals—provides the context in which the resonance of Chicano living experiences is expressed. In his use of language, the poet transgresses the recurrent
admonitions invoked by monolinguals against the mixing of languages. Montoya's use of language thus serves as a conduit for his
satirical intentions, further requiring those who enter his poetic
world to divest themselves from misconceptions they may hold regarding Chicano culture.

EL SOL Y LOS DE ABAJO

[The sun and the
  downtrodden]

Darker than most
Lighter than others—
Moreno enough not to have
Made it as an haciendado
Como Don Ramón Hidalgo
  Salazar

[Dark
rancher
Such as]

Descendant soy de los de abajo
arrastrándome voy por la vida
y arrastrado fue mi padre like
his own before—except that
mine compounded the grief by
abandoning his land for another
so foreign and at once so akin
as to be painful.

[I am of the downtrodden
I drag myself through life
My father dragged himself]

Y como él I have dragged
Myself and soul in some
Unconscious, instinctive
Search for the splendor
De los templos del sol.

[Like him

Of the temples of the sun.]

¿Y por dónde me habré
Arrastrado? Does it
Matter? Soy do los de
Abajo—find the gutters
The prisons, the battlefields,
Y los files de algodón—
Ahí me encuentran. En las
Vecindades—pronounced
Bah—rrrio now by patronizing
Do-gooders who understand
Us—or rather an image of
Us—decomposed and rearranged
Between eye-piece and lens.

[And where have I
dragged myself?
I am one of the
downtrodden

And the cotton fields
You find me there. In the
Neighborhoods]

How often have I performed
Inside that ocular tube?
I have squirmed in Logan
Heights and in Barelas.
In the fields of Fresno and
The orchards del condau de
Yuba y con La Guardia Nacional
De Nuevo México en las Filipinas

Y en las cantinas dejé mi

[in Yuba County
and with the National Guard
from New Mexico in the
  Filipines
And in the bars I left the
  flower

Primavera—en la cantina de
La China en Fowler, and the
Boulevard Tavern in Honololu—

of my youth—at the bar of the
Chinese Woman in Fowler

Y en las prisiones también—
De Chino hasta Folsom, de
San Cuilmas a la Tuna . . .

And in prisons, too—
From Chino to Folsom, from
San Cuilmas to La Tuna]

Me habré arrastrado
pero los pensamientos
de mi vida los llevo
grabados like the
etchings de Goya and
I remember those times

[I may have dragged myself
but I carry
my life-thoughts,
etched

Times that were tiempos finos—
Chavalitos laughing at Doña
Chole la ruquilla with the ugly
Hump on her back—
La curandera, bruja, life-giving
Jorobada que curó a Don Cheno
Del dolor de umbligo y la
Calentura en la cintura—la que
Daba polvitos for lovers hincados
Praying to a remarkably reasonable
God that their wives and husbands
wouldn't find out . . .

Fine times
Little kids
the hag

The healer, witch,
Humpbacked who cured
From belly-button ache and
fever at the waist—she who
gave powders to kneeling]

DIOS TE SALVE REINA Y MADRE

[GOD BLESS YOU QUEEN AND
      MOTHER

MADRE DE MISERICORDIA
ESTA VELA TE OFREZCO . . .

MOTHER OF MERCY
I OFFER YOU THIS CANDLE . . .

Virgencita, cause if my husband
Finds out, he will kill me and you
Wouldn't want him in heaven
then,
Como asesino, Dios mío . . .

Dear little Virgin

As a murderer, my God . . .]

¡BENDITO SEA DIOS!

[BLESSED BE GOD!]

Bendito eres solo cuando concedes
Milagros, otherwise your shrine
Shall be arrumbado y olvidado
Until times of need, death/grief,
Despair y los otros tiempos
pesados.
Como raíces de granos enterra-
dos—
Esos son los pensamientos que
Llevo—contradictions and
Paradoxes—that I'm not so
Sure I want to set straight . . .

[Blessed only when you grant
Miracles
neglected and forgotten

heavy times

As roots of buried boils
Such are the thoughts I have]

"Toma, Lupe, lleva este
escapulario
          que lo bendiga ese cabrón
faldillón

[Here, Lupe, take this
   scapulary
to be blessed by that skirted-
   ass

del father Kelly and tell
him to
 keep his hands to himself,
¡que ya
 tu 'apá sabe! Ah, and bring
a veladora

of

That your dad already knows!
 . . . candle

 for your brother—and the
telegram
 on the table, don't open it,
it may be
 from the war saying Toti is
dead!"
 Muchachos, come and eat!
 Después saldrán a jugar.

Boys
You'll go out and play later.]

IT'S MY TURN TO KICK THE CAN!

Rosa, te quiere mi 'amá cause
The social worker's here!
¡Dios mío! A visit from the gava!
Alcen la mesa, levanten
Esas garras . . .
Americans were always at my
House. The ones who came to
Strip my Indian flesh from me
And to crucify me with germ-
bearing
Labels more infectious than rusty
Nails . . .

[Rosa, my mom wants you

My God! . . . Anglo
Clear the table, pick up
 Those rags

AMERICANS AT MY HOUSE—

Cuando no era el probation officer
Era el councilor de las escuel,
La jura or some long haired,
Lostlamb, maveric chick offering
Us the world so she could write
Her thesis.

[When it wasn't the
It was the school's counselor
The police]

 But my dismal world was so
 much brighter! My past was
 the old barn across the
canal
 that housed a lechuza that
 screeched at night scaring
 the children porque era la
 ánima de la comadre de mi
grama.

[owl

because it was

the soul of my grama's friend]

¡OIGAN!

[LISTEN!]

My abuelita's wrinkled hands
 Would clutch a hand rolled
cigarette

[grandmother

And she would squint and lift her
Gnarled finger to her ear—¡Oigan!   Listen!
Es la ánima de mi comadre
Chonita . . .   It's the soul of Chonita, my
                                                                        friend

          And we would cringe with
fear
          and would run unashamedly
          and hug our jefitos field-   father's
          scarred limbs . . .

¿ . . . y mi jefito?   . . . and my father?

También arrastrado pero   Also dragging himself, but]
At least his noble deeds
Are enriched in ballads . . .

          EL CORRIDO DE MI JEFE   [THE BALLAD OF MY FATHER]

A caballo iba el jinete   [The rider on his horse
Se movía por los cerros   Went through the hills
Perseguido por los perros   Followed by dogs
Bien fajado su buen cuete.   With his gun by his side.]

Guerrillero de la causa   [A warrior of his own people
Nobles fueron tus esfuerzos   Worthy were your actions
No por gloria ni por versos   Neither fame nor song
Fuiste a pelear por tu raza.   Led your people's fight.]

Y ahora se encuentra tu hijo   [Now your son finds himself
En las mismas situaciones   In the same situation
Diferentes condiciones . . .   Different conditions]

          ¡Chale!   [No way!]

          My actions are not yet
worthy
          of the ballads . . . me faltan   [I lack
          los huevos de mi jefe and   My dad's balls
          the ability to throw off
          the gava's yugo de   The Anglo's yoke of
          confusión . . .   confusion]

But Chilam Balam's prophetic
Chant has been realized—and the
Dust that darkened the air begins
To clear y se empieza a ver el sol.   [and the sun begins to appear.]

          I AM LEARNING TO SEE THE
SUN.

Montoya's texts corroborate Poplack's assertion that only fluent
bilinguals are able to code switch effectively. It is also evident that
the poet addresses an in-group bilingual audience who shares his
social identity and is sensitive to the semantic nuances of English

and Spanish. His switching repertoire includes a range of standard
to colloquial English and Spanish expressions that convey determined poetic purposes. This linguistic feature provides Montoya
with choices in meaning generally unavailable to monolingual authors. Montoya's bilingualism registers the conflicts between normative values and contrasting languages and cultural world views,
adopting code switching as a strategy for his satire.

The poem is structured along three major foci of poetic experience. The narrative voice speaks in first person, but it is evident that
the poet intends to convey a larger-than-life vision that includes his
generation and, ultimately, his people's past and future. In the first
section, he represents himself as one of "los de abajo" (the downtrodden) in an obvious reference to Mariano Azuela's revolutionary
novel of the struggling Mexican masses. The life Montoya intends
to describe is that of the marginal Chicano in the United States. The
second part of the narrative concerns his memories of life in the
barrio. The insights he gains from this journey into the past allow
him to envision a future that offers hope. In the final part of his
poem, he discovers that in the strength of his elders and in the culture of his childhood lie important clues that he must decode in
order to dispel the confusion created by the dominant culture.
Throughout the poem code switching serves to highlight the complex relationship between the two languages and the two cultures as
perceived through the values and feelings of the narrative voice.

As is frequent in Montoya's poetry, English is employed to maintain a formal and distant tone. In the first switch ("moreno") the
poet has two purposes: to convey a sense of intimacy normally reserved for Spanish and to avoid repetition of the word "dark," which
in current English usage does not imply the range of hues and cultural tolerance available in the Spanish tradition. This in-group image is repeated in the second instance of code switching (*haciendado*), a colloquial term that stands in open contrast to the figure of
Don Ramón Hidalgo Salazar, whose name and title represent a class
(perhaps even a racial) distinction within the Chicano community.

The second stanza begins with the word "descendant," providing
a linguistic continuity of the English base that is maintained
throughout the poem. The next language switch, extending for more
than two lines, conveys a painful concept that would be difficult to
render in English, by claiming: "soy de los de abajo," the poetic
voice addresses an in-group audience that may prove more sympathetic to his social condition of an outcast than an equivalent (socio-
logically influenced) English phrase such as "I am of the downtrodden." Since he does not mean to depict himself solely as a

"farmworker" (*campesino*) or as part of the "working-class," labels
that might convey a restrictive meaning, he opts for the phrase "los
de abajo," thus portraying the lower class in a dignified manner that
may not have a comparable affective meaning in English. This sense
is continued throughout those lines in Spanish that refer to the difficulties encountered by the poet, his father, and "his own before."
The change into English at this point establishes a narrative distance and helps regain the composure of the poetic voice, avoiding
the danger of giving an appearance of self-pity, a sense that would be
inappropriate in a eulogy. As has been mentioned before, the continual shift between English and Spanish signals a sequence of ap-
proximation and distance that permits the poet to re-create the complex flux of the bicultural world he describes.

Two phrases in Spanish frame the third stanza; the first switch
("y como él") regains the in-group intimacy by alluding to the poet's
father; the second ("de los templos del sol") provides a majestic description that might have seemed trite if rendered in English, as well
as awkward: "of the temples of the sun." The switch into Spanish
in the last line also helps dramatize the possibility that awaits the
poet's "instinctive search" when he finally encounters his indigenous heritage symbolized in the "templos del sol."

The importance of the next passage is central to Montoya's poetic
vision: he denounces those who are incapable of fully assessing the
humanity of the downtrodden, whose redemption the poet now prepares us to discover. The initial sentence ("¿Y por dónde me habré /
arrastrado?") provides a rhetorical question that is then answered
with yet another question ("Does it matter?"). This exchange illustrates the two incompatible views the poet seeks to describe: the
perspective of those who exist in a marginal state and the normative
values under which they are judged. But a tone of defiance is also
evident, a stance posed by the narrative voice within an alien and
unfeeling environment (gutters, prisons, battlefields). The center of
Chicano life ("los files de algodón / Vecindades") is rendered in Spanish, providing a sense of cultural accuracy within the poet's linguistic experience. The insensitive outsider must first be discredited
("patronizing / Do-gooder") in order to revaluate the life of Chicanos
whose image has been distorted when studied as if he were a speci-
men in a laboratory ("that ocular tube"). These conditions allow
him only to "perform" as he and other Chicanos are confined to
squirm, projecting only an image, "decomposed and rearranged / between eye-piece and lens."

The poet leads the reader into the past through the various settings in which he had found himself as a young man. The different locations he mentions are geographic settings that encompass barrios, fields, military stations, and prisons in New Mexico (Logan Heights, Barelas), California (Fresno, Yuba County, Fowler, Chino, and Folsom), Texas (San Cuilmas and La Tuna), and abroad (the Filipines and Honolulu). English is used to create distance—he has "squirmed" in the midst of an indifferent world—but he switches to Spanish when he gets closer to the events, focusing cameralike on specific scenes.

The use of Spanish also reflects his association with other Chicano soldiers, as well as a young man's pride in being able to claim to those at home that he has been "con la Guardia Nacional de Nuevo México en las Filipinas." The socialization of the young Chicano soldier-farmworker leads him to cantinas, which are evoked through the lyrics of a popular song: "En las cantinas / dejé mi primavera" (I left the prime of my youth at the cantinas). But he fails to mention the following lines of the song he has quoted: "Me eché a los vicios / me di a la perdición" (I took the path of vice and immorality). Those lines are important here, since they suggest an underworld of delinquent activities that accounts for the large number of Chicano inmates.

His anguish at confronting a difficult life ("Me habré arrastrado") reaffirms the humanity of the poet's memory which is like an "etching of Goya." The switch from Spanish to English ("grabados like the etchings") reflects the fact that the poet has acquired knowledge of art terms in English while his emotive affinity to Goya is encoded in Spanish. This artistic claim redeems his life and projects his remembrances to an aesthetic level that parallels his ultimate search for the "templos del sol" (temples of the sun). His final switch to English in the last two lines (and / I remember those times . . .) provides continuity to the stream of consciousness maintained throughout the poem by reestablishing the narrative voice as it addresses the reader in a direct and descriptive manner.

The world evoked by the poet transports the reader to "tiempos finos," a suggestive phrase that seems a literal translation of "fine times," but which in Spanish conveys a sense of nostalgia for the richness of earlier, pristine times. The images recalled, however, are not of an innocent age, but of a community whose vitality allows for a humorous view of human frailty. Significantly, the judgmental and somber tone that the poetic voice has displayed is dropped. Having censured the attitudes that reduce Chicano life to a series of negative images, the poet can now draw upon humor when alluding to figures within the Chicano community. By so doing he moves from a predominantly satiric mode toward outsiders into a comedic tone reserved for cultural peers. In this humorous depiction of local figures, therefore, Montoya reaffirms the normative values of the Chicano community.

Through a series of vignettes, the poet re-creates in his journey to the past the images of childhood, family, and community. Young children mock the hunch-backed old woman whose status as a *curandera* (healer) places her at the center of the social landscape. The use of the diminutive *chavalitos* (young boys) and the pejorative *la ruquilla* (hag) leaves no doubt as to the affective stance of the poetic voice in relation to the other children and the ridiculed old woman. The reader is thus able to perceive the communal, internal vantage point from which it is possible to assess the full human dimension of Chicanos. Only this perspective, which stands in open contradiction to external considerations, yields an accurate vision of the drama and comedy that is human life. Subtle shades of meaning may underlie Montoya's shift from one language to another. His narrative voice employs Spanish to parody the believers' opportunistic religious fervor ("Bendito eres solo cuando concedes / Milagros"). In choosing Spanish, Montoya allows for in-group criticism avoiding a possible offensive, detached judgment from outside the group. The poetic voice returns to the present and to the reflecting consciousness of the narrator: the shift into Spanish dramatizes the emotive images of the deserted and forgotten chapels and the difficult times.

Borrowing an image from folk medicine (raíces de granos enterrados [roots of buried boils]), the poet reveals how deeply lies the source of his spiritual and social preoccupation. This simile marks one more experiential level in the poet's retrieval of essential aspects of his past: the memory of the poet has thus been likened to a Goya etching and now discloses a deeply rooted discomfort. Switching to English will, once more, help him gain distance from his feelings and redefine the situation (as "contradictions and paradoxes") as well as add a tinge of irony at his ambivalence ("that I'm not so / Sure I want to set straight").

In the narrative axis of the poem, the past is perceived from the intimacy of the home, as the mother struggles to create a psychological shelter for her children. Her strategy reveals at once an unshakable faith that gives her strength (thus the "escapulario" and the "veladora") and a realistic understanding of the dangers of the outside world. She acknowledges the immoral priest with scorn ("cabrón faldillón") and provides her daughter with the means to threaten him ("¡que ya tu 'apá sabe!") should he attempt to flirt with

her. A similar realization of life's dangers prompts her to leave un-
opened the telegram that has arrived ("it may be from the war saying
Toti is dead"); and by·delaying the confrontation of the unbear-
able pain that his death would represent, the mother helps prepare
herself and her family for the possibility for such an event. However,
by denying the possible death of the absent son, she is able to maintain the feeling that he continues to be alive and reassures herself of
his eventual return. Throughout her monologue English becomes
the medium through which the outside world is confronted ("Father
Kelly," "the war"), whereas Spanish retains the intimacy of family
life ("Toma, Lupe," "tu 'apá," "muchachos").

Having depicted the emotive disposition of the maternal figure
toward the outside world, the poet now proceeds to denounce the
external agencies that intrude into his home during his childhood.
The disruption thus implied, forcing children to suspend play
("Rosa, te quiere mi 'amá") and causing chagrin to the mother at the
unannounced visit ("Alcen la mesa, levanten / Esas garras . . ."), only
partially describes the impact of such Anglo-American ("the gava")
presence at a Chicano home. Addressing an in-group audience, the
poetic voice recounts the various agencies that sent officials to the
home ("Cuando no era el probation officer") and who brought a
sense of racial discord ("The ones who came to / Strip my Indian
flesh") or social stigma ("germ-bearing / Labels") which the poet
equates to a crucifixion "more infectious than rusty / Nails." Ultimately, the heaviest charge is launched against the aspiring academic who comes to "study" the family in order to write "her thesis." The clear implication is that this figure represents the epitome
of the "do-gooders" he had mentioned earlier, those who understand
only "an image of / Us—decomposed and rearranged / Between eye-
piece and lens." Yet the narrative voice assumes an equality with his
oppressors by displaying a Christ-like spiritual stance:

Americans were always at my
House. The ones who came to
Strip my Indian flesh from me
And to crucify me with germ-bearing
Labels more infectious than rusty
Nails . . .

The poet's journey to the past recounts, through a child's eyes, his
observations of the adult world. The reminiscence of those early
years, although "dismal," has allowed him to reestablish a sense of
personal harmony; and the wonder of the child overcomes the lamenting disposition of his embattled adult mood. The world thus

recaptured provides a rich source for the imagination and is, accordingly, "so much brighter." Even the terrors of childhood—such as the awe of the unknown and the supernatural (the Other)—may be reenacted along with the sense of protection provided by his parental figures ("jefitos"). This is symbolized by the elderly grandmother whose knowledge allows her to maintain a serenity before her departed intimate friend Chonita, whose soul, metamorphosed as an owl, screeches nearby. The recollection of these memories proves soothing to the narrative voice who confronts a present in which fears are of a social and psychological nature and have been internalized as a stigma. Yet unlike his childhood terrors, he now lacks the help of supportive elders who may alleviate his anguish. This awareness gives moral strength to the poet who can now employ English lyrically, in a celebration of his life: "But my dismal world was so / much brighter!"

Having unlocked and re-created the earliest memories of his inner family sanctuary, the poet proceeds to reassess the significance of his sociocultural experience. The image of his parents' "field-scarred limbs" has been only too painful a reminder of the dehumanizing consequences of agricultural labor. Yet the father's earlier rebellious years redeem the ensuing life of toil. The poet focuses on the heritage of epic balladry to converge the exemplar conduct of his father and the cultural ideals prevalent in the Chicano community. English is now the medium that Montoya uses to retrieve to present consciousness the blending of a dignified life ("ennobling deeds") with the imaginative interpretations of popular culture ("enriched in ballads"); Spanish serves to emphasize the emotive (the colloquial "jefito") and solidifies the bond that links father and son through a conflictive historical experience ("también arrastrándose"). In ballad form the paternal figure is eulogized with the legendary attributes of the border *corrido* hero: riding alone through inhospitable terrain while being pursued by the bloodhounds of an overpowering enemy and ready to defend himself with his pistol in his hand.

In the second stanza of the *corrido*, the poetic voice adopts a declamatory tone to recount the significance of those heroic deeds. This evaluation is retrospective and, thus, departs from the style of traditional balladry which lacks such narrative self-consciousness. Moreover, the syntax and vocabulary employed ("No por . . . ni por," "nobles," "gloria," "versos") as well as its meter and rhyme (regularly octosyllabic rather than irregular—and *abba* rather than the usual *abcb* pattern) reveal a literary rather than an oral borrowing on the part of the poet. These rhetorical clues as well as the inclusion of expressions associated with the contemporary Chicano movement ("la causa," "la Raza") suggest that the narrative has surfaced to the present in the mind of the poet.

Attempting to maintain the dignified tone of the *corrido*, the poet seems suddenly to realize the discrepancies between past and contemporary history and feels that he must stop, after apologetically attempting to rationalize his present condition. He seeks to compare his father's historical experience with his own, half-heartedly arguing that circumstances have changed ("En las mismas situaciones / Diferentes condiciones"). He brings his ballad to an abrupt halt by addressing himself and his peer group with a single negation—an emphatic and meaningful *caló* term: "¡Chale!"—as a dramatic recognition that the language of the urban underworld can provide contemporary Chicanos with the rhetorical means by which to convey an epic stance.

"El corrido de mi jefe" represents a masterful structural depiction of the psychological process that the poetic voice undergoes in attempting to reconcile his present and his past. The next stanza brings to full consciousness this fundamental conflict. It involves no less than the son's image of his father's exemplar masculinity and his own apprehension ("me faltan los huevos de mi jefe") at achieving a heroic level "worthy of the ballads." The use of Spanish signals to an in-group audience, with a sense of urgency, the need to develop a renewed epic awareness, now inhibited by psychological oppression ("the gava's yugo de confusión").

In the last stanza, the poetic voice draws from the ancient Mayan tradition ("Chilam Balam's prophetic / Chant") to reaffirm the vision that has been revealed through the journey into the past. The redemption is granted by the claim to a pre-Columbian spiritual heritage which legitimizes the historical experience of Chicanos and transcends that of the mestizo—expressed in the interplay of English and Spanish: the languages of the conquerors. In this context the consciousness of the poet announces triumphantly that only through such a process of self-discovery will Chicanos achieve their aesthetic and historical liberation.

The Epic of Marginality

In Montoya's poetry those figures that adhere to the norms of mainstream American society are the oppressive agents of a devalued world. The poet finds among the marginalized, however, an alternative series of figures who have maintained a human dimension and who, consequently, must wage a heroic struggle in order to retain their roles in life. That is, socially acceptable norms deny the virtuous their rightful role of moral, ethic, or aesthetic exemplariness. In contrast, the figures eulogized by Montoya serve as paradigms of truthfulness, compassion, love, or genius. And as culture-creators, even though poor and powerless, they provide those close to them with superior moral or aesthetic values. In the poems "*La jefita*" and "*El Louie*," for example, the two protagonists are portrayed as normative models whose strength and singularity enriched the lives of others. In both poems the poetic voice recognizes a special quality in figures and contexts that would otherwise be considered insignificant, anomalous or, worse, deviant.

"La jefita"

Jefita (little mother) is a term that combines *caló* (slang) and the affectionate ending provided by the diminutive in Spanish. It is used in informal situations to refer to the mother in the same way that the masculine, *jefito* (little father), is employed in reference to the father. Since it is a marker of non-Standard Spanish, the term is charged with meanings that allude to home and personal identity. Its usage for intimate purposes is evident in Montoya's poem, where the memories of childhood serve as a framework to evoke the figure of the mother. The poetic voice, however, is aware that this eulogy involves the danger of drawing on the firmly established notions of motherhood in Mexican and Anglo-American cultures. Since the former tends to romantic extremes and the latter often involves psychological (Freudian) perspectives, neither of the two conventions is appropriate for his purposes. In order to avoid these cultural pitfalls, he draws from his bilingual repertoire to maintain a balanced emotive basis throughout his poem. It is this careful attention to nuance that allows him to frame the praise of the mother within a working-class experience that is realistic while being emotionally charged.

The poetic voice elicits the images and sounds of migrant camps where women prepare the meal for the next day. These memories lead to the figure of the mother at work, the sound of her rolling pin, inseparable to her cough: "clik-clok; clik-clok-clok / y su tocesita." In an aside the poetic voice confides that his mother never slept. Sharing this information serves two important functions: first, it brings the reader within the circle of intimates and thus permits the poet to continue his narrative *en confianza* (with candor). A second function is to help establish the unique qualities of the eulogized figure, a portrayal that will be delicately drawn throughout the rest of the poem. The images are then recalled by the poetic voice from

the consciousness of childhood: "Reluctant awakenings a la media /
Noche y la luz prendida." A comic note avoids a melodramatic
tone while preparing the audience for the domestic informality
of the migrant's house: the boy using—and missing—the bedside
pan (PRRRRRRINNNNGGGGGG! / A noisy chorro missing the /
Basin").

An exchange between the tireless, affectionate mother and the
loving but sleepy son provides the reader with an intimate sense of
the tenderness provided by the mother:

¿Qué horas son, 'amá?	[What time is it, Mom?
Es tarde mijito. Cover up	It's late my son
Your little brothers.	
Y yo con pena but too sleepy,	And I felt bad]
Go to bed little mother!	

While the child gradually loses consciousness and falls asleep, the
figure of his mother acquires an almost mythical character, in sharp
contrast to the familiar home sounds and imagery.

A maternal reply mingled with	
The hissing of the hot planchas	[irons
Y los frijoles de la olla	And boiling beans
Boiling musically dando segunda	keeping time
A los ruidos nocturnos and	To nocturnal noises]
The snores of the old man	
Lulling sounds y los perros	[and the dogs]
Ladrando—then the familiar	[Barking]
Hallucinations just before sleep.	
And my jefita was no more.	

Early next day the mother is still found overseeing domestic
preparations:

Y todavía la pinche	[And still the damn
Noche oscura	Night is dark]
Y la jefita slapping tortillas	[And Mom making tortillas]
Prieta! Help with the lonches!	[lunches
Calienta l'agua pa tu 'apá	Boil water for your dad]

In sharp contrast is the father figure, who awakens the family with
an irritating whistle and unkind words: "Arriba, cabrones chavalos,
/ Huevones!" (Get up, you rotten, lazy kids). Once more, the poet

assures us that his "jefita" never slept, and yet she would work next day in the fields picking her share of cotton.

> Y en el fil, pulling her cien   [And in the field, . . . hundred
> Libras de algoda . . .   Pounds of cotton]

This maternal figure fulfills her duty selflessly and with love and care. The son, as the narrative voice, conveys his concern for her well-being: "Go to bed little mother!" In his feeling there is also compassion and despair because conditions require her to overwork, and he is helpless to prevent it: "y yo con pena but too sleepy." The poetic voice conveys a feeling of rebellion toward the father, a figure whose role the narrator-son is condemned to imitate in adult life. This situation does not leave room for a comparison between the father and the mother representations. While both parents adhere to traditional custom, within their roles they convey their individual characters: the father is an authority figure demanding and distant, while the mother is supporting and tender. The contrast between their respective personalities is synthesized in the last line of the poem: such is the strength and generosity of this woman that even the father, who can be tough and sarcastic, pays her the highest normative compliment: "That woman—she only complains in her sleep."

"El Louie"

Montoya encodes the transition from a rural to an urban culture among the people of Mexican descent in the United States during an important historical period: the late 1940s and the early 1950s. In this poem the narrative voice recounts the life and deeds of Louie, a significant figure among his young peers in a Chicano community. This sociohistorical dimension, however, only accounts partially for the poem's success. "El Louie" is an artistic creation of multifarious resonances due to the manner in which the poet is able to synthesize essential aspects of the Chicano experience. That is, the poem conveys the perspective of working-class youth through their linguistic, psychological, aesthetic, and social conventions.

In his eulogy the narrator levels criticism against the barriers that have limited Louie's life. There is an implicit censure of the restrictive norms imposed on his vitality and courage after he has demonstrated his heroism. His ultimate defeat, however, is posited as the tragic flaw of a local boy whose promising talent remains unfulfilled. Thus, in counterpoint to the charismatic Louie, whose leadership sets the tone for an epoch and a generation, stand the destructive forces that account for wasted intelligence and the tragedy this represents. In lamenting Louie's unfortunate death, the poetic voice emphasizes the positive aspects of his life—judging it to be "remarkable." Yet in order to recognize him as exemplar, it is necessary to avoid a strict adherence to orthodox values and behavior. This is why disregarding the solemnity of the occasion—a funeral oration for a fallen hero—the poet proceeds to violate the conventions of the genre and introduces language considered abusive (*pinche:* lousy) and unconventional (*vato de atolle:* a cool dude). This departure from propriety ought to be a fundamental consideration in any interpretative approach to the poem, since its meaning and emotional tone depend on the delicate balance maintained between Louie's nonconformist behavior and the encomium of his life.

The forceful nature of Louie's character is evident immediately: he will cause an upheaval whether his destiny in afterlife is heaven or hell:

Hoy enterraron al Louie	[They buried Louie today
And San Pedro o San Pinche	And Saint Peter or Saint Devil]
are in for it . . .	

The significance of his death is thus measured by the potential his life represented. To his eulogizer Louie's threat to the established order—whether it be to a heavenly guard or to his devil counterpart—is sufficient cause for admiration. This assessment is sustained by calling him "un vato de atolle" (a cool dude), a judgment based on the premise that only an internally based collective sense can serve as a final arbiter in the evaluation of its members. Accordingly, symbols of respectability imposed from external sources—be they religion, class, or social etiquette—are elements of a repressive system, and defying them is an ethical imperative to those whose loyalty rests primarily within the group.

The life of Louie is presented to the reader through a fragmentary, fast-paced succession of events that help delineate his personality. We learn that he was a prominent figure among young Chicanos in San Jose, California (Sanjo). One of his most memorable traits was his "fantasy" to play the roles of popular film figures. Louie's role-playing, however, must be judged in light of the poet's particular appreciation of the hero's imaginative mind. He is a charismatic youth, whose ingenuity, courage, and aesthetic sense represented lasting influences on his generation. In his portrayal of Louie, how-

ever, Montoya does not wish to sound overly dramatic and half-
jestingly imitates the epic musical background of films:

> And Louie would come through—
> melodramatic music, like in the
> mono—tan tan taran!— . . .   [movies]

In the central and most extensive section of the poem, the reader
is lead by the poet through a close recounting of Louie's times and
deeds. The social and geographic context that Montoya re-creates
includes small farmworking communities predominantly in the San
Joaquin Valley—from Fresno to Gilroy and San Jose—an agricultural
region populated substantially by people of Mexican origin. Throughout this Chicano migrant network, los Rodríguez (young Louie and
his brothers Candi and Ponchi) were well known. At the peak of his
adolescence, Louie was in an enviable position: he drove a fancy car,
was well-dressed (*buenas garras:* literally, "good rags"), was popular
with the girls (*rucas:* literally, "old ladies"), and was seen playing
his guitar *(liras)* and singing popular Mexican songs ("La palma").
His ingenuity led him to design *pachuco* clothes or zoot suits
("tailor-made drapes") an idea his peers found "unique" because of
Fowler's distance from the centers of Chicano cultural activity—Los
Angeles ("Los") and El Paso ("E.P.T," the legendary birthplace of the
pachuco). Such a contented figure evoked by the poet conveys a rare
inside view of a Chicano community—generally perceived by outsiders negatively and, stereotypically, in terms of poverty and devi-
ance—but which provided a lyrical setting for the vivacious group
headed by Louie.

The relationship between the narrative voice and the protagonist
becomes apparent in the sixth stanza, as the former recounts the
influence exerted by Louie on his immediate circle of friends and
relatives. To his followers, among whom the narrator is included,
local events compensated for the distance and isolation they felt
from the life-style and fashions available in large urban centers ("the
big time"). Within this context Louie served as a fulcrum for the
group's activities ("we had Louie"). Thus, at the slightest sign of an
upcoming conflict, the group would turn toward Louie for direction
("get Louie"), and under his command they quickly responded and
organized. In a Chicano version of epic conflict, the poet describes
the young warrior as he assembles his troops:

> "Ese, 'on ta 'l Jimmy?"   ["Hey, where's Jimmy?"
> "Orale Louie."   "Right here, Louie."
> "Where's Primo?"   "Where's cousin?"

"Trais filero?"   "Have you got a knife?"
"Simón."   "Yes."]

In this chaotic scene, bravery is depicted against the background of fear from the girls ("No llores Carmen, we can handle them" [Don't cry Carmen]) and the group's censure of those unprepared to fight ("¿Trais filero? / Nel. / Ooh, ese bato." [Have you got your knife? / Nope. / Get out of here]). The battle must occur in a secluded place away from the hated and ever-present police ("la jura"). Throughout such events Louie finds his most glorious moments ("he would come through") as the urgency of the situation enabled him to display his inclination toward role-playing ("he dug roles"). But the seriousness of the experience ("gut-shrinking, love-splitting, ass-hole-up-tight bad news") is counterbalanced by the fictionalized performance of Louie ("melodramatic music and all"). The poet portrays Louie's stylized sense of life through the roles offered by Mexican ("Cruz Diablo, El Charro Negro") and American media heroes ("Bogart, Cagney, Raft"). While conjuring the memory of Louie, the poetic voice brings to mind Louie's bent on imaginative personifications:

"Ese Louie—"   [Hey, Louie—
"Chale man, just call me 'Diamonds'!"   No]

Louie's fate leads him to the U.S. Army, where, keeping in character, he demonstrates his courage ("con huevos": with courage, literally, with balls). But in spite of his heroic actions on the battlefield, his rebellious nature brings him into predictable conflicts with the military authorities ("paradoxes . . . / heroism and the stockade"). In his visits home, the image of a new Louie—donning a military uniform—impresses the community:

And on leave, jump boots
shainadas and ribbons, cocky   [shined]
from the war, strutting to
early mass on Sunday morning.

The response among young and adults is equally admiring of Louie's martial figure, and he enjoys a newly gained respectability:

"Wow, is that ol' Louie"
—¡Mire, Comadre, ahí va el hijo de Lola!—   [Look, Comadre, there
                                                 goes Lola's son!]

The returning veteran soon enters a phase of decline. In contrast to his earlier promising image, in his adult years Louie is to suffer the effects of a demoralizing and destructive world. It is indeed an irony that "at barber college he came / out with honors," in reference to Louie's chosen occupation during a period that offered Chicanos few socioeconomic opportunities. And this figure, who once deployed what seemed a mythical leadership, is now unable to engage in some ordinary struggles. He is seen pawning his military decorations ("bronze stars") and hair-cutting tools ("velardo de la peluca" [haircutting case]) in exchange for liquor ("pisto") and gambling money ("para jugar pocar serrada and lo ball" [to play poker and low ball]). The tragic figure of "Legs Louie Diamond," whose fate deprives him of realizing his earlier promise, eventually sinks to lower levels and "hit[s] some lean times." In keeping with the decorum of the funeral oration, the poet does not explicitly mention Louie's drug addiction, merely alluding to him as: "kind of slim and drawn there toward the end," and "He died alone in a rented room—." This strategy allows Montoya to emphasize the positive aspects of Louie's life and to suggest only that a tragic turn ultimately caused his demise.

The poetic voice will repeat twice a lament for the fallen hero before bringing the elegy to closure: "Hoy enterraron a Louie" (They buried Louie today). It will be the younger *pachucos* ("baby chooks") who now recall Louie's deeds ("cuando lo fileriaron en el Casa Dome y cuando se catió con la Chiva" [the time he was knifed at the Casa Dome and when he fought with the "goat"]). It is an appropriate homage, since these young Chicanos assembled at the pool hall—a public forum of Louie's own—recount his memorable deeds. This testimony from the next generation helps corroborate the poet's praise of Louie's extraordinary nature.

Throughout the poem the narrative voice assumes that his status as a peer has allowed him to recognize the remarkable and heroic quality of Louie's life. The reader is thus invited to listen to this voice empathetically in order to do justice to the tone and meaning of the poem. But establishing rapport with someone like Louie might involve a considerable effort—especially if the reader is unsympathetic to Mexican working-class youth culture. Indeed, many a reader may feel uninclined to accept the epic or tragic portrayal of a figure that could be considered socially marginal, even threatening. In the Western canon, such a situation may, at best, be represented as a mock epic. It is clear, however, that Montoya's purpose is not to scorn or deride Louie. Within Louie's own frame of values, his death "alone in a rented room" is a tragedy. It is a funeral scenario demeaning to such a formidable figure. A man who deserved an epic death:

No murió en acción—
no lo mataron los vatos
ni los gooks en Corea.

[He didn't die in action
he wasn't killed by someone in a Chicano gang
neither by Asians in Korea.]

In a final lyrical concession to the deceased hero's imaginative nature and dramatic sense, the poet envisions the manner in which Louie must have carried himself during his final moments, displaying the stoicism, bordering on indifference, of some of his cinematic heroes ("perhaps like in a Bogart movie"). That Louie's death is "a cruel hoax" because his life had been "remarkable" is thus an aesthetic resolution to the problem that Montoya faced in "El Louie": praising an extraordinary youth, a born leader, whose charisma, ingenuity, and imagination are ultimately defeated by a restrictive and dehumanizing environment.

The reader may be tempted to interpret Montoya's poetic voice either as a spiritual or as an existentialist vision, deeply imbued with an evangelical—Christian or pre-Columbian—inclination, or else as the political product of the 1960s, with a current of ethnic cultural nationalism. His upbringing in Roman Catholic New Mexico, with strong native American ties, was certainly a major influence in his orientation. Similarly, Montoya's values were shaped by extensive reading of modern philosophical and literary texts. His orientation to U.S. society was undoubtedly inspired by his experiences at Berkeley during a time of intense ideological ferment. While there is no doubt that Montoya has received a number of these and other influences, his poetic aspiration seems directed primarily to the faithful interpretation of Chicano life.

Montoya's poetry focuses on a series of incongruencies in life, satirized from the perspective of a Chicano normative alternative. In a comic undertone, his narrative voice wages a spirited affirmation of Chicano culture and values. This undertaking is articulated through a poetic persona who, in a series of asides directed at the reader, conducts a running commentary on the admirable characters portrayed; adopting now an air of self-mockery, feigned astonishment, or resigned helplessness. It is an attitude that allows the poet to shift, often surprisingly, from seriousness to frivolity—and vice versa—while maintaining control over the mood of his poetry. Montoya is thus able to sustain a critical stance toward prescriptive norms while drawing his audience to a position from which to appreciate his poetic perspective and his sharp wit.

In his depiction of Chicano characters, Montoya alludes to their plight but does not belabor the causes nor the agents of discrimination, thus avoiding the type of polemic that would make the satiric target a central theme of his poetry. In his work, therefore, the representation of Anglo-Americans occupies a secondary or minimal role. Montoya's attitude is consistently compassionate but rarely descends to an anguished lamentation for suffered deprivations. He avoids falling into self-pity or the possibility of diminishing the inherent strength or beauty of those figures and themes that he presents in positive terms. A delicate balance is thus maintained in which the struggle of modest but admirable characters is portrayed affectionately while their efforts to survive in a chaotic world are depicted heroically. The poet's underlying attitude can be characterized as a humanistic or spiritual concern for the most essential values that render life worthy of respect.

A satirical vein informs Montoya's poetry and serves as a counterpoint to the positive representations of the community life that he has chosen to portray. Drawing from his immediate family and community circle, he sings of the vicissitudes and triumphs of humble figures whose aesthetic tendencies and moral determination defy conventional norms. But in a materialistic and opportunistic world, such defiance will bring fatal consequences to the rebels, especially to those who, as Chicanos, already occupy marginal positions. The spiritual and aesthetic values of exemplary figures are thus counterposed to the madness posed by contemporary irrationality in an uneven contest: the former are admirably superior though socially defenseless; the latter maintain a dominant position but deserve contempt. Thus, throughout his poetic corpus, Montoya exalts outstanding figures whose role is to provide love, dignity, imagination, and beauty in the midst of a callous, dehumanizing environment that encroaches on Chicano life.

4. Rolando Hinojosa: Klail City Death Trip Series

The novelistic project of Rolando Hinojosa—known as the *KCDTS*, or Klail City Death Trip Series [1]—encompasses seven published volumes to date.[2] Although it may appear that each book stands as an independent unit, the narrative coherence evident throughout Hinojosa's novels supports Rosaura Sánchez' observation that they make up "a unitary text with a macrostructure within which are articulated microstructures (that is, the individual volumes)" ("From Heterogeneity" 76). This narrative unity is organized along a series of complex stylistic features such as multiplicity of narrators and characters, fragmentation of time, and variability of point of view—in addition to the blending of diverse literary, folkloristic, and historical discourses.[3] Yet the narrative's apparent simplicity may puzzle readers who first enter the aesthetic world of the fictional Belken County.

Yolanda Broyles suggests that in *Klail City y sus alrededores* "we are invaded by a feeling that the townspeople are in truth speaking for themselves instead of being narrated" (119). This impression of collectivity is particularly evident in the Spanish narratives (*Estampas del valle, Klail City y sus alrededores, Claros varones de Belken,* and *Mi querido Rafa*). In contrast, the works written in English, where the settings portrayed are primarily non-Chicano (*Korean Love Songs, Rites and Witnesses,* and *Partners in Crime*), convey a markedly different effect, as the two protagonists, Jehú Malacara and Rafa Buenrostro, gradually distance themselves from activities in the Chicano community and enter into an Anglo-American public sphere.[4]

Following the literary tradition of Mark Twain, García Lorca, and Juan Rulfo, among others, Hinojosa renders the grammar and modulation of popular speech into writing. Although Hinojosa accomplishes this task apparently with little effort, it is a difficult balancing act that requires translating oral conventions into literary terms, a procedure that involves reinterpreting the functions and values of variant artistic and social contexts. This transit from one discourse to another in the *KCDTS*, however, requires familiarity with those conflicting planes of discourse at which the Anglo and Mexican cultures meet. Such exchanges involve a debate over alternative normative values, and in the imaginary world of Belken County—as is wont to occur in other cultures—the debate is expressed through comic or satiric discourse. Only someone like Hinojosa, a lifetime participant and observer of a traditional border community, would be capable of registering the cultural complexities implicit in the tales of Klail City.[5]

Hinojosa's varied literary indebtedness, however, must not be disregarded. The invention of an imaginary Belken County, for example, is a thinly disguised attempt to represent the Mexican communities of the Lower Rio Grande Valley of Texas, in the manner of Faulkner's Yoknapatawpha County. Hinojosa has acknowledged his admiration for Faulkner in unequivocal terms: "Anyone who writes is going to have to read Faulkner," and he credits the Mississippian for his own inspiration to write: "When I read *The Unvanquished*—which in some ways parallels what I am doing with the Mexican Revolution in my work, as well as the coming together of different cultures here—I saw what I wanted to do later on" (Saldivar, *Hinojosa Reader*). There are also references to a great variety of authors and works in many languages.[6]

A plot in literary fiction, as a self-contained entity, ought not require readers to go beyond textual boundaries in order to recover essential aspects either in the meaning or in the motivation of its characters; it would indeed represent an authorial failure to omit essential clues in a narrative.[7] In the Belken County saga, however, plots and characters at the surface level appear fragmented, disconnected, and incomplete. But this is only a postmodernist appearance. Rather, as Broyles has pointed out, it is an attempt to imitate traditional culture: "In a strongly oral culture, locutions are not linear but circular: spoken words happen in many places at the same and at different times, but they recur. They return from mouth to mouth to revive a life experience, an event. . . . The medium is memory and the instrument is voice. Memory both constitutes and transmits culture" (120).

The role of the reader in the *KCDTS* (or the reader of any literary text) is largely that of a mute receptor of textual flow, unlike audiences of traditional genres who customarily engage in a give-and-take exchange with oral performers. Therein lies a central distinction between literary and oral transmitters; the fundamental experience of oral folk is dialectical: in helping shape their tradition they are informed by that tradition, and as carriers and transmitters of local history they are actively engaged in its preservation (Ong 41). In adapting the speech conventions of oral culture to his narrative, Hinojosa provides the reader with relevant pieces of information. That is, whereas in a traditional setting, it is assumed that the listener possesses sufficient data to interpret the meaning and significance of the events and characters, the reader in the *KCDTS* becomes a semioral receptor acquiring essential information by methods resembling those employed in oral performance.

In a tight-knit oral community, mnemonic procedures help maintain a sense of history and self-identification (Leal, "History" 102). Family chronologies and genealogies help to identify important characters and to assess the significance of the events in which they participate. A sense of collectivity, thus, is re-created by Hinojosa through a multiplicity of characters whose interrelated lives are subject to public scrutiny. The reader, therefore, must play a role similar to that of an observer in a traditional (oral) culture who is simultaneously a witness, a judge, and a jury in an incessant public normative game.

The narrative begins as Jehú Vilches, grandfather of Jehú Malacara, muses on the request of his son-in-law-to-be, Roque Malacara, for his daughter's hand in marriage. Vilches recalls his own experience years before when as a young man he stood before his father-in-law-to-be, Braulio Tapia, to ask for the hand of his wife, Matilde. Vilches wonders, "¿A quién vería don Braulio en el umbral cuando él pidió a su esposa?" (I wonder whom did Don Braulio see when he asked for his own wife?) (*EV* 16). The reader will discover the answer to this rhetorical question later on:

> Braulio Tapia, natural de El Esquilmo (ahora Skidmore) Texas, nació en agosto de 1883; a Braulio lo criaron Juan Nepomuceno Celaya y una tía materna, Barbarita Farías de Celaya, ambos de Goliad, Texas. . . .
> Braulio apareció en lo que ahora es Belken County en 1908 y se casó dos años después con Sóstenes Calvillo, hija única de don Práxedis Calvillo y Albinita Buenrostro. De éste matrimonio nació Matilde; ésta se casó con don Jehú Vilches y tuvieron una hija, María Teresa de Jesús, que se casó con Roque Malacara. (*EV* 122)

> [Braulio Tapia, originally from El Esquilmo (now Skidmore), Texas, was born in August 1883; Braulio was raised by Juan Nepomuceno Celaya and a maternal aunt, Barbarita Farías de Celaya, both from Goliad, Texas. . . .
> Braulio first arrived in what is now Belken County in 1908 and two years later married Sóstenes Calvillo, only child of Don Práxedis Calvillo and Albinita Buenrostro. This marriage had an offspring, Matilde;

she married Don Jehú Vilches, and they had a daughter, María Teresa
de Jesús, who married Roque Malacara.]

As can be expected, the elders are the keepers of collective memories. This explains the impatience on the part of the aging peers of
Cipriano Leal when he fails to recognize the names of well-known
local people:

> ¿Quién es ese muchacho, Genaro?
> Se llama Rafa Buenrostro.
> ¿De cuáles Buenrostro?
> ¿De los de Julián?
> No, éste es de Jesús Buenrostro al que llamaban don Jesús.
> Ah, sí; murió joven.
> ¿Ese fue el que trabajó con el viejo Burns?
> No. Ese fue Julián. Don Jesús tenía unas tierras cerca del Carmen.
> ¿Donde se echaron a los rinches?
> Ahí mero.
> Ya, ya. A don Jesús le decían El Quieto.
> *¿El Quieto?*
> Sí; újule Leal tú ya no te acuerdas de nada. (*EV* 50)

> [Who is that boy, Genaro?
> His name is Rafa Buenrostro.
> From which Buenrostros?
> From Julián's?
> No, he is the son of Jesús Buenrostro whom they called Don Jesús.
> Oh, yes; he died young.
> Is that the one who worked for Old Man Burns?
> No. That was Julián. Don Jesús had some land near El Carmen.
> Where they messed up the (Texas) Rangers?
> Right there.
> OK, OK. Don Jesús was nicknamed "The Quiet One."
> *The Quiet One?*
> Yes; wow, Leal, you don't remember anything.]

This dialogue between Echevarría, Castañeda, and Leal, at the
cantina of Lucas Barrón, El Chorreado, is a good example of the oral/
literary techniques employed in the *KCDTS*. Hinojosa blends the
various speaking voices without identifying the speakers; instead,
the context indicates the identity of each contributor to the conver-
sation. Such exchanges convert the readers into quasi-oral listeners,
embedded in a community context that provides congruence and
helps enhance the background and character of Rafa Buenrostro. It
is a technique also employed in re-creating pertinent data on the
uprooted life of Jehú Malacara:

> Ah, ése es Jehú Malacara.
> ¿De los Malacara de Relámpago?

Esos meros. Este es de Roque el que se casó con Tere.
¿La de las maromas?
No, hombre. La de las maromas era Peláez, hija de don Camilo y doña Chucha. La madre de este muchacho era hija de don Jehú Vilches.
El yerno de Don Braulio Tapia.
Andale . . . ya caigo.
¿Tú conociste a don Braulio, Echevarría?
Cómo no, aunque yo era mucho más chico.
Este muchacho trabajó con los Peláez en las maromas y lo medio crió don Victor.
Buena persona, don Victor. (*EV* 50)

[Oh, that's Jehú Malacara.
Related to the Malacaras of Relámpago?
That's right. This boy is Roque's, the one who married Tere.
The one from the circus?
No, man. The one from the circus was a Peláez, daughter of Don Camilo and Doña Chucha. The mother of this boy was daughter of Don Jehú Vilches.
The son-in-law of Don Braulio Tapia.
OK . . . I get it.
Echevarría, did you know Don Braulio?
Sure I did, although I was much younger.
This boy worked in the circus with the Paláezes, and Don Victor almost raised him.
Don Victor was a good man.]

Hinojosa's employment of oral devices in the structure of his narrative is particularly evident when he re-creates humorous verbal exchanges between narrators and listeners. Thus, a man nicknamed "El Turnio" ("Cross-eyed") repeatedly interrupts Jehú Malacara while the latter recounts the latest events and personalities in the community. Jehú counterattacks by ridiculing the heckler and in this way is able to maintain control of his narrative voice:

Punto por punto. Primero, don Epigmenio era de lo más huevón y tanto que por no trabajar no se echaba una querida; segundo, como me vuelvas a interrumpir, Turnio, te voy a dar tal patada en el culo que te voy a enderezar la vista. ¡Estamos? A propósito, Turnio, esto es entre paréntesis y no nada personal. ¡Pásame la sal! (*CVB* 139)

[Point by point. First, Don Epigmenio was so lazy that he would not get a mistress 'cause it was too much work; second, if you interrupt me again, Turnio ("Cross-eyed"), I'll give you such a kick in the ass that I'll straighten your eyesight. Alright? By the way, Turnio, this is beside the question and don't take it personally: pass the salt!]

This fierce mock threat advises Turnio of the annoyance his interruptions are causing. The seriousness of the threat, however, could alter the mood of the audience, and Jehú quickly dispels this possibility by interjecting a humorous incongruity (pass the salt!) that allows the narrative to continue without a change in mood. More lively interventions by the audience occur when Echevarría narrates his stories. Often the old man is aided by his listeners, who help quiet down the interruptions.

—Ustedes jovencitos no saben nada de nada.
—¡Echevarría está pedo!
—Pedo, sí, pero con mi dinero.
—No se deje, Echevarría . . .
—Hombre, no le hagan pedo, no lo choteen.
—Sí, hombre, déjenlo que siga. (*KC* 23)

["You youngsters, you don't know anything."
"Echevarría is drunk!"
"Yes, drunk, but with my own money."
"Let them have it Echevarria . . ."
"Come on, man, don't mess with him, don't kid him around."
"Yeah, man, let him talk."

These examples, and many others in the *KCDTS*, demonstrate the way in which, in oral discourse, the presence and participation of the audience is an integral part of the narrative; attempts to interpret the dialogue, removed from its context, violate fundamental aspects of its tone, significance, and meaning. Yet Hinojosa's novels remain literary creations, an irony considering that as readers we are required to forgo literary conventions in order to comprehend the reconstruction of an oral world (Broyles 127–130).

In spite of a seemingly fragmentary narrative, the *KCDTS* maintains an internal coherence, and the traditional world re-created suggests that its tales are part of a larger, inexhaustible repertoire of narrative interrelationships. That is, as in oral life, events and characters may be amplified or minimized by the narrator, and each episode is an expression of a set of shared meanings that determine the significance of the individual tales. This social coherence provides oral raconteurs with an endless source of material on which they can draw to suit their narrative purposes. Thus, theoretically, the totality of a community's events, told by all of its storytellers, forms an interdependent oral narrative web. The listener is required to focus on the characters in the narrative from the perspective of the community's standards rather than—as is customary in the modern novelistic tradition—centering on an individual's private experience that is to be measured according to normative values shared between author and reader. This collective sense helps explain the relative homogeneous nature of traditional cultures; since normative values are continuously encountered, internalized, and expressed, the individual is forced to measure all acts and motivations according to community standards.

Comic and Satiric Figures

Hinojosa employs a number of humorous strategies, such as parody, irony, sarcasm, caricature, and other rhetorical devices that involve play, incongruity, and exaggeration. As a general rule, the characters he creates share a common trait: they are unable to perceive their own shortcomings while their foibles seem outrageous to those who recount their stories and, it is assumed also, to the readers of the *KCDTS*. These figures help provide a context whereby the values of Belken County, the character of its individuals and their actions, are subjected to continuous and diverse interpretations by the various narrative voices.

Epigmenio Salazar is a man who has not worked since World War II due to a physical impediment that earns him the dubious title of "El Caballero de la Hernia" (The gentleman of the hernia), in an obvious and malicious reference to novels of chivalry and Cervantes' parodic use of similar titles in *Don Quijote*. His wife, Doña Candelaria Mungía de Salazar, also known as "La Turca" (the Turkish woman), because of her Lebanese descent, is a domineering figure who oversees the household and the income generated by her properties. In spite of the firm control that his wife exerts over him, Epigmenio manages to lead a busy though useless life, occasionally pilfering money from the household budget for his personal expenses. He spends his time gossiping about the inhabitants of Klail City and knows, for example, "lo que hay entre don Javier y la Gela; conoce de buena tinta lo que hay entre el cocinero de 'El Fénix' y la chica de la farmacia; sabe, por vías fidedignas, lo que le pasa a la esposa del menor de los Murillo" ([knows] of the relationship between Don Javier and Gela; is also knowledgeable of what is going on between the cook of "El Fénix" and the girl at the pharmacy; and a good source has informed him what is happening to the wife of the youngest of the Murillos). Yet, regarding his own affairs, Epigmenio is totally unashamed of being inactive or of the nickname that Doña Candelaria has given him: "mi huevón" (my lazy bones) (*KC* 77).

A number of cuckold figures appear in the *KCDTS*. Don Orfalindo Buitureyra, occasionally seen at the local bar singing and dancing by

himself, nevertheless maintains a sense of dignity. He refuses to re-
cite poetry or give speeches, claiming that that is only done by
"queers" (*KC* 108). Other figures are treated less kindly: "La caba-
llona" (The mare), in addition to being lazy, is considered the laughingstock of Relámpago after the response he gave when told that his
bride-to-be had slept with every man in town: "¿Y qué? ¿Qué tan
grande es Relámpago?" ("So what? How big is Relámpago?) (*EV* 177).
In contrast, "Menor" Murillo is perceived with a mixture of pity and
scorn by the townsfolk. It was "Menor" who asked his prospective
father-in-law if he could test his girlfriend before marrying her, a
request the father of the girl answered by saying that "he had not
raised his daughters to be tried out like watermelons." "Menor" is a
tragic fool who displays an insolent attitude while apparently being
the only one in town who ignores the infidelities committed by his
wife (*EV* 178).

Melitón Burnias is the protagonist of comic episodes borrowed
from the stock of folk tradition. He portrays a picaresque figure who
suffers indignities because of his meager resources. Poor Burnias, for
instance, has been driven from his own house by his daughter and
son-in-law and is now forced to sleep in the cab of a truck. In another
episode Burnias and Bruno Cano search for a buried treasure, an adventure in which both are portrayed as foolish and greedy. Burnias,
partially deaf, misunderstands his accomplice and, frightened, runs
away leaving Cano trapped inside the treasure hole. Their treasure
hunt has a tragicomic result, since Cano, also frightened and then
angry at being left behind, dies inside the hole he has dug. In another
tale Burnias is cheated of a pig he has raised to make some money.
The pig, given to Burnias by Old Man Chandler in payment for work
done, is found to have worms when submitted to a federal inspec-
tor's test, thus requiring the owner to dispose of the infected animal.
Burnias is saved by Martín Lalanda, his business partner, who inge-
niously devises a stratagem to recover their investment. Lalanda
suggests that they sell the pig back to Chandler and, should he re-
fuse, give it to him as a gift:

> Poooos, la verdad no entiendo. Es fácil: un regalo no se rechaza y éste
> menos, porque si lo rechaza tenemos que preguntarle por qué y ¿qué
> cara va a poner? Así es que tiene que comprarlo . . . En efecto, el viejo
> Chandler se vio acorralado y soltó los veintisiete del alma que le pidie-
> ron. (*EV* 135)

> [Weeeell, I just don't understand. It's easy: he can't reject a present, espe-
> cially this one, because if he rejects it we'll have to ask him why, and
> what is he going to say? So he'll have to buy it . . . It was true, Old Man

Chandler saw himself surrounded and dished out the twenty-seven
bucks they asked of him.]

In this scene Old Man Chandler portrays the figure of the trickster
who is in turn tricked by his victims.

Tomás Imás is a Protestant preacher whose assimilation of Anglo-
American customs and language serve as a source of humor. Brother
Imás is the proverbial *pocho*. Jehú describes him as an outsider to
the Belken community, observing "ese modo de estarse de pie sin
cruzar los brazos o sin estar con las manos en la cintura" (his manner of standing up, without crossing his arms or putting his hands
on his waist) (*KC* 35). Although he is later portrayed as an endearing
character (*CVB* 77–83), initially the figure of Brother Imás is ridiculed by Jehú and Edelmiro Pompa. The boys notice this Chicano
preacher who, incongruously, speaks Spanish with a heavy English
accent:

> —¿Es usté cura?
> —No, yo ser hermano predicador.
> —Es usté aleluya?
> —Shst, h'mbre, no seas tan bruto, Edelmiro.
> —¿Pos qué tiene que ver?
> —Yo ser predicador de la palabra providencial perpetua.
> —Es aleluya, Jehú. (*KC* 36)

> ["Are you a priest?"
> "No, I be brother preacher."
> "Are you an alleluia?"
> "Psst, man, don't be so rude, Edelmiro."
> "So what?"
> "I be preacher of holy providential word."
> "He's an alleluia alright, Jehú."]

Brother Imás, a Chicano from the Midwest, is a dominant English
speaker who has learned Spanish from two Anglo ministers while
training for evangelical work at a Protestant school. His stilted Spanish is mentioned ironically by Jehú:

> El hermano Imás aprendió su encantador español allí y lo primero que
> hizo fue volver a Albion para hablar en español con sus padres. El her-
> mano contó que los viejos quedaron encantados. No hay por qué du-
> darlo; yo también me quedé de una pieza la primera vez que le oí.
> (*KC* 44)

> [Brother Imás learned his charming Spanish over there and the first
> thing he did was to go back to Albion and speak Spanish with his par-

ents. Brother Imás said that his old parents were amazed. There is no
reason to doubt it, that was also my reaction the first time I heard him.]

The portrayal of false religious attitudes is yet another frailty depicted comically in the *KCDTS*. For example, while the Chicanos
from Klail City are respectful toward the Roman Catholic priest,
Don Pedro Zamudio, he is considered an irascible old man whose
pride and unyielding sense of propriety blind him to the human
weakness of his parishioners. Thus, Father Zamudio, on his way to
mass at dawn, finds Bruno Cano trapped inside the treasure hole and
is enraged when the insolent Cano demands to be taken out:

> —¿Qué pasa? ¿Qué hace usted allí?
> —¿Es usted don Pedro? Soy yo, Cano. Sáqueme.
> —¿Pues qué anda haciendo Ud. por esta vecindad?
> —Sáqueme primero. Más al luego le cuento.
> —¿Se golpeó cuando se cayó?
> —No me caí . . . ayúdeme.
> —Sí hijo, sí; ¿pero entonces como vino a dar allí? ¿Seguro que no está
> lastimado?
> —Segurísimo, señor cura, pero sáqueme ya con una . . . perdón.
> —¿Qué ibas a decir, hijo?
> —Nada, padrecito, nada; sáqueme.
> —No creo que pueda yo sólo; estás algo gordo.
> —¿Gordo? ¡Gorda su madre!
> —¿Mi quééééé?
> —Sáqueme ya con una chingada. ¡Andele!
> —¡Pues que lo saque su madre!
> —¡Chingue la suya! (*EV* 36)

> ["What happened? What are you doing there!"
> "Is that you, Don Pedro? I am Cano. Get me out of here."
> "But what are you doing in this neighborhood?"
> "Get me out first. I'll tell you later."
> "Did you hurt yourself when you fell?"
> "I didn't fall . . . help me."
> "Yes, son, yes; but then how did you end up there? Are you sure you
> are not hurt?"
> "I'm certain, father, but get me the . . . out of here, sorry."
> "What were you going to say, my son?"
> "Nothing, father, nothing; get me out."
> "I don't think I could do it alone; you are kind of fat."
> "Fat? Your mamma is fat!"
> "My whaaaaaat?"
> "Get me the fuck out of here. Come on!"
> "Let your mamma get you out!"
> "Fuck yours!"]

This dialogue is an excellent illustration of the rhetorical devices
employed by traditional storytellers. The incongruity in the tone

and the timing employed by the two speakers—one calm and inquisitive, the other quick and urgent—creates a tension that is finally resolved in a comic explosion. The portrayal of the priest as an unyielding moral figure is further demonstrated when he refuses to bury the deceased Cano, who dies, presumably of a heart attack, inside the treasure hole. The stubborn and offended Don Pedro is depicted as a failed religious leader whose anger toward the disrespectful Bruno Cano is stronger than his sacramental obligation to pray for the dead.

> Don Pedro tuvo que aguantarse y rezó no menos de trescientos Padrenuestros entre Aves y Salves. Cuando se puso a llorar (de coraje, de histeria, de hambre, vaya usted a saber) la gente, compadecida, rezó por don Pedro. (*EV* 37)

> [Don Pedro had no recourse and prayed something like three hundred Pater Nosters between Holy and Hail Marys. When he started crying (due to anger, hysteria, hunger, who knows why) the people, compassionately, prayed for Don Pedro.]

Another comic religious figure is that of Brother Flores, a member of the Mexican Baptist church. One of his most notable shortcomings, in addition to his laziness and sexual passion, is to ignore the basic religious principles of his church. He believes that Martin Luther is the Antichrist and is confused when told that Baptists are also Protestants. Jehú, now an assistant in the Baptist church, attempts to correct Brother Flores' theological contradictions. It seems, however, that Brother Flores is more concerned with access to convenient facilities at the church than he is with theological issues.

> El Hermano Joaquín Flores seguía con sus dudas. "Ni pa' qué mentirle, Hermano Malacara: esto de la religión está algo confuso. Cuando yo era Pentecostés, la cosa era más fácil: allí todos—menos los servidores y demás creyentes—allí, como decía, allí todos los demás se iban derechitos al infierno, y de narices. ¿Usted me entiende? Bien. Lo que no tenían era un piano como éste que tenemos aquí. Así da gusto Hermano . . . (*CVB* 69)

> [Brother Flores was still doubtful: "I won't lie to you, Brother Malacara: this religious thing is kind of confusing. When I was a Pentecostal, things were easier: there everybody—excepting the servants and other believers—went straight to hell. You know? Good. They just didn't have a fine piano like this one we have here. Now, that makes you feel good, Brother.]

In spite of the many characters represented in comic fashion, an undercurrent of compassion is always present toward most of the Chicano inhabitants of Belken County. While they may possess negative traits, there is deep respect for the unsung struggle of their daily existence. The preface to *Klail City* is clear about this: "Verdad es que hay distintos modos de ser heroicos. Jalar día tras día y aguantar a cuanto zonzo le caiga a uno enfrente no es cosa de risa" (It's certainly true that there are various ways of being heroic. Working day in and day out and tolerating whatever fool happens to cross your path is no laughing matter) (*KC* 12). In a similar vein, the reader is warned against grandiose notions of the human condition: "El que busca héroes de la proporción del Cid, pongamos por caso, que se vaya a la Laguna de la Leche" (Whoever expects heroes of the stature of El Cid, for example, can go to the [legendary] Lake of Milk) (*KC* 11–12). Thus, because Epigmenio Salazar is perceived as a "chismoso, sinvergüenza y gorrón" (gossip, shameless, and parasitic), at his funeral his wife must disguise her deep affection for him (*KC* 79). While Don Orfalindo is known as a *cabrón*, following the etymological sense of the word (*cornudo:* cuckold), he is also considered an inoffensive, though pathetic, figure by the bar patrons who leave him to his eccentricities (*KC* 108–112). Burnias, who is the laughingstock of the the town because of his destitution and simplemindedness, receives an honest and appreciative welcome when, breaking all precedents, he buys a round of beer at the local bar (*CVB* 107). In spite of Brother Imás' linguistic inadequacies he earns the respect of those Chicanos he seeks to convert (*CVB* 83). Father Zamudio and Brother Flores are ridiculed for their spiritual shortcomings, yet their characters, like other humorous figures in the *KCDTS*, are comic because they do not pose a danger or a threat to the survival of the community.

The Bakhtinian notion of the disintegrated personality, whose alienation produces an individual existing solely for himself, appears in Belken County as a satiric figure who is estranged from his community. An example of this is Adrián Peralta, a *coyote* or trickster figure who hunts the halls and offices of city buildings in search of innocent monolingual Spanish-speaking Chicanos, to whom he offers "help" in exchange for a few dollars. Peralta's callous and exploitive nature is evident in his demeanor:

> Trigueño, sombrero de petate a la moda, camisa blanca y corbata con ganchito de donde salta un pez vela, sonrisa en la boca que no en los ojos, bigote fifí, con ese par de ojos mencionados que si no han visto todo poco les falta. Como tiene la piel curtida ya no le entran ni indirectas ni insultos. Tiene buena presentación y mejor voz ya que hasta la fecha nadie le ha rompido las narices. (*EV* 131)

> [Light skinned, a fashionable straw hat, white shirt and a tie with a small hook from where a sailfish jumps out, a smile on the mouth but

not in the eyes, a mustache *fifí* style, with that pair of the abovementioned eyes which have seen everything or almost everything. Because he has a thick skin, no hint or insult gets to him. He has a good presentation and even a better voice, since no one has yet broken his nose.]

Another comico-satiric example is Packy Estudillo, the aging car thief whose alienation is the product of a low-level intelligence. After spending forty years, alternating the life of a convict with that of the delinquent, Packy has not learned much and leads a meaningless existence consisting of a series of recurring mistakes (*PC* 202–205). Rather than projecting the frightening and dangerous image of the criminal, or the sad but sympathetic and romantic figure of the convict, Packy is portrayed as mentally deficient. His role combines that of the delinquent in modern postindustrial society with that of the fool: a deviant with social and psychological problems. His institutionalized frame of mind is evident when, about to be apprehended, Packy's immediate reaction is to doubt his sanity:

> Staring at the ceiling, he noticed that some of the paper was beginning to come off; but, he thought, it's been like that for four years.
> He then said: "What I need is a lawyer."
> And then, almost in the same breath and behind that thought, a new one: "No; what I need is one a-them psychiatrists. That's what I need."
> "I must be crazy," he went on. "But it's my fault." (*PC* 210)

As an agent of the corrupt Leguizamón family, Polín Tapia is portrayed as an unprincipled politician who seeks the favor of the banker Noddy Perkins and the Anglo establishment. Polín is characterized as a servile flatterer; his fundamental insincerity is evident in the stream-of-consciousness monologue he conducts as he approaches the bank:

> Was that the Bewley girl I waved to? Why did she give me a funny look? Was I moving my lips? Got to watch that. . . . First thing you know, people'll think you're crazy; worse, they'll think you're silly. . . . What's that? Me! My reflection; glass case in pocket; tie straight; belt . . . shoe . . . there she is again; opening the door. Must've been expecting me.
> "Good afternoon, young lady." (*RW* 22)

Another target of satire is Big Foot Parkinson, an Anglo sheriff whose linguistic eccentricities and false claims of affection for the Mexican community denote him as an outsider and a hypocrite. Big Foot is the proverbial gringo. While campaigning for office in the Chicano community, he demonstrates his utter foolishness. Among the skeptical members of the community, there is little favor either toward his candidacy or the motives of his Chicano supporters:

—Yo casar primera vez con mujer jacana pero ella voy por murio.
(Aplausos)
—Yo volver casar y yo casar otra vez mujer jacana y ella voy por
murio.
(Más aplausos)
El Big Foot seguía a la carga:
—Yo casar tercer vez con mujer jacana y ella también voy por murio.
Aquí, siempre, y sin fallar, venía el choteo:
—¡Las estarás matando de hambre, animal!
—¡Es que no te aguantan, colorao!
—¡Te apesta la boca!
La raza comprada y vendida aplaudía y hacía *sh, sh,* para mostrar que
ellos, a lo menos, eran educados. (*KC* 52)

["I marry first time Chicana woman but she go died."
(Applause)
"I marry again Chicana woman but she go died again."
(More applause)
Big Foot continued his speech:
"I marry third time Chicana woman but she go died again."
At this point the jokes would always start:
"You are probably starving them to death, you beast!"
"They just can't live with you!"
"It's because you have bad breath!"
Only the sell-outs would applaud and say "*sh, sh,*" to show that they,
at least, were educated people.]

In the *KCDTS* a number of characters represent a threat to the
hegemony of the Chicano community. Historically, the underlying
conflict in Belken County has been over the land first acquired by
the Mexican founders of the area and the legal subterfuges used by
the English-speaking newcomers who deprived the rightful Spanish-
speaking heirs of their property. Those Chicanos who joined the Anglos in this conflict are depicted as traitors. A principal target of
satiric treatment are the Leguizamón, their descendants, and their
clients. Whereas other satirized figures may be portrayed somewhat
comically, indicating their relative inoffensiveness, the depiction of
characters such as Javier Leguizamón, Becky Escobar, and her husband, Ira, is definitely of antagonists for whom there is little sym-
pathy. It is evident that the satire on the Leguizamón family is
grounded on the image they represent, as allies of the KBC ranch
and as representatives of the loss of property, traditions, and values
in the Chicano community:

La historia de esta familia o familión es bien conocida: llegaron tardía-
mente al Valle y viendo cómo corría el agua, se hicieron primero mexicanos viejos, luego pasaron como españoles y por fin patriotas: esto
último no quiere decir que sirvieron en las armas del país. Hay otras

maneras de ser patriotas: hacer dinero; joder al prójimo, acomodarse
a lo vigente, en fin: irse por el camino trillado. (*CVB* 145)

[The story of this family or family conglomerate is well known: they
were late arrivals to the Valley and seeing how things worked here, first
became Old Mexicans, then passed as Spaniards and finally became pa-
triots: this does not mean that they served in the armed forces. There
are other ways to be patriotic: make money; screw your fellow man, fit
into the status quo, in other words: take the well-traveled road.]

The corruption of the Leguizamón is deep, and its demoralizing
effects are noticeable on the sibling relationship of the two surviving
members of the family.

De los cinco que hablamos sólo quedan dos, Antonia y Javier. Como en
todas familias, hay un poco de todo. Estos dos ni se ven ni se hablan.
Creo que la Antonia no quiere acordarse de su sangre chicana pero eso le
ocurre a muchos y qué le vamos a hacer. Javier no es chicano tampoco,
es Leguizamón y los Leguizamón, bien es sabido, no tuvieron madre;
fueron hijos de tía.

[Of the five we have mentioned, only two are still alive, Antonia and
Javier. As with all families, there is a little of everything. These two
don't see or talk to each other. I think Antonia doesn't want to be
reminded of her Chicano blood, but that happens to many people, and
what are you going to do about it. Javier isn't a Chicano either, he is
a Leguizamón and a Leguizamón, as is well known, is motherless; they
all are children of aunts.]

Yet, the festering moral and social decay in Belken County is most
evidently found among the members of the Klail-Cook-Blanchard
family and their associates. Their catalog of vices includes dishonesty, alcoholism, murder, greed, and sexual promiscuity. These faults
are hardly questioned socially or prosecuted legally because of the
priviledged status they hold as the owners of most of Belken County.

Rafa Buenrostro and Jehú Malacara: Hero and Anti-Hero

The respective cognomens of the two central characters in the
KCDTS, Jehú Malacara and Rafa Buenrostro (bad face and good
countenance) are an indication of a polarity, reflected in their respective attitudes toward life. Jehú is an extrovert who is resource-
ful, ironic, and controversial, while Rafa, an introvert, has a balanced, endearing, and gracious personality. Jehú's name suggests his
biblical counterpart, the combative elected king of Israel. The many
biblical allusions and quotations throughout the narrative indicate
that Hinojosa borrowed more than names. The resonances of the

name Jehú are indeed rich, since the biblical Jehú defeats the corrupt Ahab and destroys the sinful Jezebel, a moral act of great import in the Judeo-Christian tradition.[8]

In contrast, Rafa's name (a nickname for Rafael) suggests both the archangel who leads Tobias and the Italian painter considered an artistic pillar of the Renaissance due to his sense of harmony, movement, and delicacy. Rafa is indeed an exemplary figure possessing some of the qualities most esteemed in the traditional world of Belken: knowledge, loyalty, generosity, gentleness; and his actions convey modern attributes: decisiveness, competence, ambition, and accomplishment. Another pertinent parallel may be made with Rapha, a biblical figure whose name means "he (God) has healed," an allusion that could refer to Rafa's physical and moral wounds: the assassination of his father, the death of his young wife, and his ordeal in Korea.

Rafa has grown within the shelter of his extended family and has received the prestige the Buenrostro name has among the Chicanos of Klail City. In contrast, Jehú, lacking the support of his immediate relatives, has survived by his wits. As a child, Jehú was given shelter by the Buenrostros, but this was not an act of charity, since they considered him part of their extended family (*RW* 50). Both cousins spent their childhoods as orphans and, in spite of their respective differences, remained intimate friends throughout life. But whereas Jehú's disintegrated family structure and precarious subsistence has helped shape his satiric orientation, the protection of a family circle gives Rafa an outlook based on stability and generosity. Upon his return from Korea, Rafa reminisces nostalgically upon his formative years:

> . . . al abrir un cajón del armario vi el retrato de mi tía Matilde Buenrostro. Como casi no conocí a mi madre, llamé "Mamá" a mi tía; hermana de mi padre, ella dirigía nuestra casa que era algo parecida a la de los Vielma en limpieza y orden y también en cierto ambiente. No había la rigidez de los Vielma pero sí la misma paz. Los problemas en casa se pensaban; no se oían gritos a ninguna hora. (CVB 189)

> [. . . while opening a dresser drawer I saw the photograph of my aunt Matilde Buenrostro. Since I hardly knew my mother, I called my aunt "Mama"; she was my father's sister and ran our household, somewhat resembling the Vielmas' in cleanliness and order and also a bit in atmosphere. We weren't as rigid as the Vielmas, but we did have the same peacefulness. In our house problems were thought out; you never heard any yelling.]

There is a fundamental contrast in the lives of the protagonists: Jehú is the uprooted; and Rafa has solid family and community ties.

This distinction is critical to understanding the context in which Rafa and Jehú grow up. Within the norms of a traditional society, such as that of Belken County, family and personal identity are closely intertwined, and the status of an individual is determined, to a large extent, by interpersonal loyalties whose source begins at the family nucleus. This affective and social paradigm, therefore, is structured along a series of concentric circles that begin with the nuclear family and move away in decreasing order of importance toward the extended family, friends, and associates, community, and other people with similar characteristics that may include culture, class, gender, age, and regional origin. The normative framework of the *KCDTS* thus replicates the various loyalties that have helped shape Chicano history.

Rafa Buenrostro, like Jehú, descends from a lineage that founded Belken County in the eighteenth century, and his family's experience symbolizes the resiliency demonstrated by a people during a difficult historical period. He is the inheritor of heroic tradition in a region where cultural conflicts have been expressed through a corpus of balladry. It is thus not a coincidence that the lands of Rafa's father are named "El Carmen," a place "donde se echaron a los rinches" (A. Paredes, *With His Pistol* 226), in a clear reference to the *corrido* of "Gregorio Cortez" and the Texas Rangers.[9] The murder of Rafa's father, Don Jesús Buenrostro, "El Quieto," posits an ethical commitment on his family who, according to tradition, must avenge the crime. The response of his next of kin is a mixture of grievance and rage, a reaction that serves as motivation for the brother's revenge:

> Habían matado a don Jesús Buenrostro mientras dormía y su hermano don Julián, casi se volvió loco de rabia . . . sin avisarle a nadie, don Julián, sólo, cruzó el río en busca de los que habían matado a su hermano.
> Volvió a poco más de mes y parecía un hombre que estaba en paz con todo el mundo. (*KC* 53)

> [They had killed don Jesús Buenrostro while he slept, and his brother Don Julián was so furious he almost went crazy . . . without telling anybody, don Julián, alone, went across the river in search of those who had murdered his brother.
> He returned in a little over a month and seemed to be a man who was at peace with the world.]

The revenge Don Julián exacts for his brother's murder frees Rafa from the responsibility that he would have otherwise inherited. Nevertheless, Rafa appears to have an epic mantle that casts a shadow over his life. Although it is not explicitly stated, there is every reason to believe that the Anglo establishment was aware of the events surrounding Don Jesús Buenrostro's death. After all, Alejandro Leguizamón's plot to kill Rafa's father was certainly known—and approved—by Big Foot Parkinson, an agent of the Klail-Cook-Blanchard family, a fact not likely to be withheld from the centers of power (*KC* 31). Yet Rafa, perfectly aware of the conflicts between his family and the ruling families of Belken, appears ready to let the past lie.

In spite of his misfortunes—the loss of his mother as a child, the assassination of his father, the drowning of his young wife, and the physical and mental afflictions he suffered as a soldier in Korea—Rafa's conduct demonstrates positive normative values: he is consistently judicious, compassionate, loyal, and courageous. Furthermore, he demonstrates cultural loyalty toward his community and is personally concerned for the well-being of other Chicanos. Thus, for example, he demonstrates his closeness to the Chicano community through the genealogical knowledge that allows him to engage in intricate conversations with his elders:

> Doña Barbarita conoció a mi padre siendo ella unos pocos años menor que él: "Sí, lo conocí bien. Asuntos de familia, como te podrás imaginar; nosotros y los Campoy siempre nos vimos bien. De los Vilches ni hablar, yo casi me crié allí ellos y por eso conozco estas tierras tan bien como cualquiera. ¿Te acuerdas de la noria de agua salada?"
> "¿De la que está cerca del monumento, dice usted?"
> "No, esa no, más acá. ¿Tú conociste a los Bohigas . . . ? en esa familia a todos les abultaban los ojos."
> "Sé quienes son pero nunca los conocí . . . perdieron las tierras allá por Bascom a los Leguizamón, ¿verdad?"
> "¡Diablo de muchacho! ¿Pero cómo te acuerdas tú de esas cosas?"
> (*CVB* 181)

> [Doña Barbarita knew my father; she was a few years younger than he: "Yes, I knew him very well. Family business as you can imagine; the Campoy family and us were very close. I don't have to tell you about the Vilches; I almost grew up with them; that's why I know those lands as well as anybody. Do you remember the saltwater well?"
> "You mean the one near the monument?"
> "No, not that one, closer over here. Did you know the Bohigas? Everyone in that family had bulging eyes."
> "I know who they were, but I never met them . . . they lost land near Bascom to the Leguizamón, didn't they?"
> "Darn child! How can it be you remember those things?"]

Rafa's characteristic generosity leads him to give away his inherited land to old family allies. Upon his return from Korea, Rafa brings presents and comfort to the families of his buddies who had died on the battlefront. From one of them, he receives their highest accolade when he is compared to his father:

> "Mil gracias, muchacho."
> Estaba con el pañuelo en la mano cuando salieron las muchachas; las chaquetas les encantaron pero el retrato del hermano mucho más."
> "¡Qué bien salió Chalillo!"
> "Eres un sol, Rafa. Un sol."
> "El espejo de tu padre." (*CVB* 179)

> ["A million thanks, boy."
> He was holding a handkerchief when the girls came out; they liked the jackets but were even more pleased with the picture of their brother.
> "Chalillo came out very well!"
> "You are a ray of sun, Rafa. A ray of sun."
> "The living-image of your father."]

Rafa's qualities serve him well as a member of a new generation of Chicanos who are professional, educated, and upwardly mobile. In Korea he earned a bronze star, and the GI Bill allows him to earn a bachelor of arts and, subsequently, a law degree. He goes on to become the first Chicano teacher at the Klail City High School and in the latest novel to date, *Partners in Crime,* is employed as a detective for the Belken County Homicide Squad. The delicate balance that he must maintain in order to tread between two conflicting worlds—one representing his past, the other his future—does not appear to be a dilemma for Rafa. This is due, to a large extent, to his personality which, like that of his father's, is characteristically reserved.

The portrayal of Rafa, as a soldier in Korea and later as a detective in Belken County, suggests the image of the modern popular American hero who appears reticent and unemotional when acting on a moral principle. This appearance, however, is only external, since, as heroic characters, these two American popular figures, the soldier and the detective, lack "round" personalities. In Rafa's case this external quality is expressed in the portrayal of events and characters that define his life rather than, as is customary in the modern novelistic tradition, as a self-awareness that helps explain his motives and actions. But such an internal psychology, a product of modern alienation, would be only partially valid for a Chicano from Belken whose traditional upbringing accentuates the collective over the individual. Rafa thus is an idealized version of the Mexican American as an individual able to achieve a smooth cultural transition into the mainstream of Anglo-American life without losing the richness of the Mexican cultural heritage. As a normative figure, he represents an alternative to the dual cultural world he confronts, a situation that is echoed in the words of Matthew Arnold that serve as the epigraph to the English translation of *Klail City* (*The Valley* 9): "Born between two worlds, one dead and one as yet unborn."

Hinojosa does not aspire merely to transpose an oral into a writing mode but to attain an artistic reelaboration of traditional culture. This literary purpose is evident in Jehú's picaresque existence, which includes a number of conventional features such as the death of his parents at an early age and his subsequent initiation into a life of wandering while holding various occupations—in a circus, as an altar boy, as a preacher's assistant, a bartender, an officer in a bank—under a variety of masters who are often depicted in satirical terms. Jehú is able to overcome his destitution because of his natural intelligence and the help of a succession of protectors, a few of whom—such as Don Victor Peláez and Don Manuel Guzmán—become substitute paternal figures.

Jehú's ironic frame of mind has been evident since early childhood. After his father's death, he visits some of his cousins and reflects on the ridiculous behavior of his aunt:

> La cosa es que así que sepultamos a papá, a mí me dejaron solo esa tarde y no teniendo más qué hacer fui a casa de la tía Chedes para ver a mis primos. Cuando la inútil de mi tía me vio empezó a llorar y a hacer sus papeles. . . . Al rato se le quitó el llorido y se quedó con el hipo sempiterno; como la pobre era tan bruta, luego luego me preguntó que qué andaba haciendo por la vecindad. Por poco me echo a reír, pero me detuve y le dije que venía a jugar con mis primos. (*EV* 19–20)

> [What happened was that once we buried Dad, they left me alone that afternoon, and since I didn't have anything to do, I went to Aunt Chedes' house to visit my cousins. When my worthless aunt saw me, she started to cry and act up. . . . Soon she stopped crying and kept the customary hiccups; since my poor aunt was so stupid, she asked me right away what I was doing in the neighborhood. I almost burst out laughing, but I held back and told her I had come to play with my cousins.]

Jehú subverts the role of his aunt as an authority figure by caricaturing her emotionalism and her superstitious tendencies and by pointing out her lack of tact toward him. He maintains a sober, distant judgment even as he describes his own humorous reaction to her absurd and foolish figure.

An important satirical axis of the *KCDTS* is commanded by Jehú whose role will be to depict many of the comic figures of Belken—thus helping reinforce the normative values of Mexican traditional society—and to devalue the satiric targets he censures. This is especially evident in the sarcastic undertone of Jehú's letters in *Mi querido Rafa*. In this volume Jehú works at the Klail City First National Bank, where the young clerk learns that power is maintained through manipulation and that the reins of social and political influence are in the hands of the corrupt. He shares his discovery with Rafa, one of the few individuals in Belken who shares his understanding of the false values that Jehú must confront. Jehú's description of the leading Chicano and Anglo citizens is of moral destitutes who feign respectability, a situation that becomes the subject of his systematic mockery. Although Jehú considers himself to be on a superior moral level, his personal situation is precarious because of his reluctance to participate actively in the devious games played by his employer. Jehú's depiction involves an inversion to the role of the *picaro*, who rises economically but descends morally and is a willing participant to dishonesty. The main target of his censure is the KCB family whose representative, Noddy Perkins (also Jehú's boss), ruthlessly safeguards their interests.[10] The mental ordeal Jehú must withstand to fulfill his duties at the bank represents a series of tests to his subservience: "With Noddy you never know. Now, I do know some things I shouldn't, and I now wonder if Noddy knows I know . . . no, no, that way lies madness" (*MQR* 35).

This cat-and-mouse game described by Jehú will be presented, in *Rites and Witnesses*, from the perspective of various observers of Jehú's actions at the bank, including the rich Anglos. Behind his humor, Jehú's letters reveal a deep concern for social and ethical values and roles; a central motif is the assessment of moral character according to degree of cultural loyalty demonstrated by Chicanos.

In contrast to Ira Escobar—whose foolishness is only equaled by Big Foot Parkinson, the Anglo sheriff—the conduct of Jehú is guided by a sober assessment of the strict limitations under which he must work at the bank. Ira, an ambitious Leguizamón, becomes one of the central targets of Jehú's ridicule because of Escobar's naiveté and unfamiliarity with traditional Mexican culture. Thus, Jehú portrays Ira as incapable of engaging in the verbal dueling (*choteo*) that is frequent in male gatherings:

Allí estaba Ira con un RC Cola en una mano y taco de tripas y servilleta en la otra. Contó un chiste muy viejo y luego lo contó de nuevo, esta vez en inglés y salió mejor: esta vez se rieron unos bolillos. . . . Como el pobre de Ira carece de sense of humor, luego luego Santana y Segundo de la Cruz se le echaron encima, le tronaron tres o cuatro en un minuto y la risotada se oyó hasta el otro lado del Río. (*MQR* 24)

[There was Ira with an RC Cola in one hand and a tripe taco and a napkin in the other. He told an old joke, and then he told it again, in English; this time it came out better: a few Anglos laughed. . . . Since poor Ira lacks a sense of humor, immediately Santana and Segundo Cruz got on his case; they pulled about three or four gags in one minute, and the laughter could be heard all the way to the other side of the Rio Grande.]

Escobar's transgressions of rural Chicano conventions reveal him as a comic figure of foolish proportions. He thus eats tripe tacos while drinking a soda pop (and holding a napkin!) rather than the accustomed beer, indicating his concern to be "moderate" and "clean," hardly necessary in an informal situation and with food not associated with genteel manners. Furthermore, his failed joke reveals linguistic incompetence and dullness. That he opts to repeat the (old) joke in English exposes his firm intent to participate in the ongoing discourse without realizing that he has breached the Chicano cultural homogeneity at an ethnically mixed gathering. His success in provoking the laughter of the Anglo guests informs Ira's position as a marginal figure whose faux pas is rebuked immediately by verbal assaults on the part of other Chicanos. But it is Jehu's interpretation that prevails in the comic portrayal of Ira's behavior. That is, Ira is depicted as a Chicano who ignores some fundamental conventions of his people, and his failure to participate as an equal in a Chicano ritual renders him as a clumsy peer. Implicit in this condemnation is the awareness of Ira's self-perception as urbane and sophisticated—in this context an offensive normative principle involving class, race, and ethnicity—a notion that renders his figure an appropriate target for satirical attack.

Jehú's disdain of Ira is centered on the latter's lack of political savvy that blinds him to the evident fact that his candidacy is ruthlessly manipulated by his financial supporters, the dispensers of power in Belken County. Ira enters the political race under the false impression that it is merit, rather than his usefulness to the KCB ranch, that renders him a viable candidate. Other equally gullible Chicanos are willing to support Ira, believing in a rigged electoral system. Yet the fraudulent quality of Ira's candidacy is obvious to Jehú: "Te diré esto: la raza está convencida que 'Ira's their man' and the bolillada that 'Ira's their boy' " ("Let me tell you: Chicanos are convinced that 'Ira's their man' and the Anglos that 'Ira's their boy' ") (*MQR* 27). From his position at the bank, Jehú is able to observe how Ira falls prey to the astute Noddy Perkins: "Ira todavía no puede entender que la elección es un cinch; todavía cree que *algo* va a pasar. Noddy doesn't know what a good job he did on Ira . . . WHAT

AM I SAYING? Of *course* he knows. He just enjoys seeing Ira hop, is all" (Ira still cannot understand that the election is a cinch; he still believes that *something* is going to happen) (*MQR* 42).

Because Ira lacks the most elementary understanding of the reality of Belken County, he is a pitiful victim who actually believes himself to be superior. His simplicity is such that he ignores, for example, that the KCB ranch exerts complete political and economic control over the lives and fortunes of the Belken people.[11] Thus, Noddy Perkins is obliged to warn Ira regarding the political role he is expected to play:

> Noddy lo sentó y entonces le explicó, en esa voz, ce por be cómo corría el agua en Belken; que quién se encargaba de las compuertas; que quién era el señor aguador; que quién decidía a cuáles acequias se les daba agua y a cuáles no; y cuánta agua y también cuándo; y etceterit y etceterot. Así. Noddy habla de agua pero hasta el más lerdo sabe perfectamente de *qué* se está hablando. (*MQR* 38)

> [Noddy sat him down and then explained to him, just like that, A to Z how water was allocated in Belken; who was in charge of the flood gate; who was the waterman; who decided what irrigation ditches to fill and which not to fill; how much water and when; and etceterit and etceterot. That's it. Noddy speaks of water, but even the dullest person knows exactly *what* is being said.]

The scope of Jehú's difficulties as a Chicano working for the Klail City First National is best illustrated by the guarded relationship he has with his boss, Noddy Perkins. The Anglo manager, believing in the talent of his young trainee, has advocated Jehú's promotion before the KCB family council. Jehú's relationship with the Buenrostros has been a matter of concern in his appointment, and the young banker feels he is watched. The old conflict regarding the murder of Rafa's father is discussed by Noddy, and Jehú's cautious answer to his boss reveals the distrust he has for the motives behind Noddy's inquiry:

> "Did you ever know Quieto? I mean, do you remember him, Jehú?"
> "No, not really; not when I think about it, anyway. I was still a kid then . . . That was close to . . . what? Twenty years, by now?"
> "Just about. You understand we had nothing to do with that, right?"
> "That's why I'm here . . . "
> "What do you mean, Jehú?"
> "I mean I wouldn't come to work here if I thought . . ."
> "Yeah?"
> "If I thought that the KCB had *anything* to do with his death, Noddy."
> "I know you wouldn't. . . . Look, I don't even know what made me say

what I just said. . . . Okay? Reassurance of some sort, I guess . . . I mean, my own reassurance."
"Rafa hasn't forgotten." (*RW* 50–51)

The love affair with Sammie Jo Perkins, Noddy's daughter, represents a dangerous step that may cause Jehú the loss of his position at the bank. In Belken County such interethnic relationships, when they occur, are usually between Chicanas and Anglo men but are relatively rare between Chicanos and Anglo women.[12] Furthermore, Sammie Jo's status as a married woman involved with a Chicano looms as a possible scandal that is certain to embarrass the KCB ranch. In his characteristic fashion, Noddy invites Jehú to a dinner at his house and proceeds to dismiss him in a ceremony intended to publicly dishonor him.

> *Ya habían cenado todos para cuando yo llegué.* Llegué a las ocho (the time set for dinner by Noddy) y el asunto tomó menos de tres minutos, tops.
> Becky no levantó la vista (the whole time), los Terry ni chistearon (no surprise there) & Ira was studying the Utrillo on the wall. An art lover, yet.
> Noddy made it short: "Jehú, I recommend that you resign as loan officer." (*MQR* 45)

> [*They had already dined when I arrived.* I got there at eight (the time set for dinner by Noddy) and the matter took less than three minutes, tops.
> Becky didn't raise her sight (the whole time), the Terrys didn't blink an eye (no surprise there) and Ira was studying the Utrillo on the wall. An art lover, yet.
> Noddy made it short: "Jehú, I recommend that you resign as loan officer."]

Next Monday morning Jehú arrives at Noddy's office to discuss his situation:

> Entonces, yo, que me agarraba de chorros de agua para detenerme, lo atajé:
> "Does my firing have to do with sex, Noddy?"
> Se me quedó viendo por un rato larguísimo (his favorite ploy) y luego explotó:
> "You Mexican son-of-a-bitch." (*MQR* 46)

> [Then, I, trying desperately to hold on to a water stream, stopped him:
> "Does my firing have to do with sex, Noddy?"
> He looked at me for a long time (his favorite ploy) and then exploded:
> "You Mexican son-of-a-bitch."]

Jehú, desperate to avoid an unseemly dismissal, must outwit the Machiavellian Perkins. His strategy consists of (1) admitting to a lesser transgression—his affair with Becky Escobar, Ira's wife; and (2) claiming with feigned outrage that his relations with Ollie San Esteban, his girlfriend, are of no concern to Noddy. In so doing Jehú gains credibility to support his denial of the true cause for Noddy's anger: the affair with his daughter Sammie Jo. This tactic then renders convincing his apparent surprise when Sammie Jo's name is mentioned:

> "Ollie? San Esteban? I'm talking about Sammie Jo, goddamit!"
> "Sammie Jo? You've got ahold of some bad shit there, Noddy."
> "*Bull*shit."
> "Bull*shit*. Lets call her—better still—let's you and I go on out there. Goddamit."
> "You . . ."
> "Hold on, Noddy. You *know* I'm telling the truth . . . It's something *else*, isn't it?"
> Of course, the man was absolutely right. But he was bluffing. (*MQR* 46)

Noddy's defeat is a symbolic debasement of the KCB. The sexual conquest of one of the clan's women represents a mockery to their legitimacy as forgers of Belken's social respectability and questions their political preeminence. The fact that Noddy, the representative of the ranch and its political engineer, is incapable of manipulating Jehú, demonstrates the vulnerability of the forces that control the lives and fates of the Chicano inhabitants of the region. While this violation does not constitute a major threat to the ranch's power, within the evaluating framework provided by Jehú, their symbolic defeat is unquestionable. Satiric discourse attempts such victories by undermining the assumed invulnerability of normative values held by an opposing group. It will treat figures identified with positive values as "the Other," thus subverting them into negative or marginal figures. In his function as satirist, Jehú targets (1) those figures, such as the Leguizamón, who are alienated from their cultural heritage and community roots and act as the agents of community outsiders; and (2) the dominant group, the KCB ranch, and all those who infringe upon the success of Chicanos or the realization of their cultural objectives.

Jehú's extended monologue in his letters to Rafa parallels what Claudio Guillén labeled as a "spoken epistle" to describe the narrative voice in *Lazarillo de Tormes* ("La disposición" 266).[13] *Mi querido Rafa*, however, may be considered picaresque *sensu lato* as are other novels in European literature that alter the strict adherence to a picaro protagonist.[14] Jehú's figure is that of a sarcastic narrator who exposes the deceit of others. That is, as a picaresque character in Belken County, Jehú is unable to engage in a wide range of questionable acts. He will not proceed as did Lazarillo, who "first surrenders himself to a corrupt world and afterwards ironically redefines it as Utopia" (Gilman 161). Such behavior would bring Jehú uncomfortably close to the figures he satirizes and who are indeed unaware of their own degradation. Instead, his character is legitimized by the positive figure of Rafa, whose presence in the background validates the norms under which Jehú's satiric voice launches a pointed attack throughout the *KCDTS* narrative. In turn, the intimate friendship between the two cousins softens the normative character of Rafa, suggesting a sense of his human dimension. These positive qualities are absent among the satirized who abide by values that are rigid, dishonest, and removed from those customarily found among the Chicanos of Belken.[15]

In nontraditional communities (best exemplified by postindustrial Western societies), an individual's economic, social, and psychological role is relatively autonomous from the family, the peer group, and the community. The assimilation of the two protagonists in the *KCDTS*, Rafa Buenrostro and Jehú Malacara, into an alien world where their activities are not regulated by the conventions of the Chicano community—that is, Anglo education, English language, the armed forces, and their respective jobs at the bank, the high school, and the police force—illustrates the shift from a traditional to a nontraditional evaluative framework. Yet the separation of the two protagonists from other Chicanos is not portrayed as an alienation, since both maintain their loyalty toward Chicano culture and, consequently, are able to maintain their dignity, a quality highly prized among the Chicanos of Belken County. This positive aspect of their roles reinforces the normative paradigm of the Chicano community.

In order to trace this shift from a social to a private psychology, Hinojosa's novels employ oral and literary conventions. As descendants of the original settlers of the region, both Rafa Buenrostro and Jehú Malacara are intimately tied to its history. They grew up within a traditional world where a predominantly collective sense informs all events in the lives of its people. This cultural cohesiveness, once characteristic among Chicanos, leads the two protagonists to structure their lives according to two fundamental principles: (1) the normative values they have inherited as members of the Chicano community and (2) the demands that a modern, alien world places on them. The implications of this transformation touch on virtually every aspect of human existence, but it is fiction—and especially the novel—that is ideally suited to convey such complex historical conditions. In the monumental *Klail City Death Trip Series*, two protagonists and hundreds of characters, through satiric discourse, re-create literarily the cultural existence of an entire people.

5. Conclusions

I have favored approaching Chicano literary culture as a historically evolving discourse that interfaces with various cultural traditions and is notable for its combative (epic) stance—in the manner Américo Paredes proposes in his works on folklore—rather than as a recent epiphenomenon of elegiac (tragic) tendencies—as suggested by Juan Bruce-Novoa for poetry. Thus, my satirical analysis addresses the particular situation that Chicanos have confronted since the nineteenth century, when their lives were subjected to alternative normative codes. Yet given the juncture at which we presently are in the research of Chicano literary culture, this study has necessarily been a selective introduction on Chicano satire and satirists.

Satire may have seemed an incongruous genre to emphasize in a study on Chicano literary culture. Satire, on the one hand, is generally identified as a genre in creative texts that are part of a firmly established literary tradition and have impeccable linguistic, historical, and aesthetic credentials. Chicano culture, literary or otherwise, on the other hand, is customarily considered an expression of "the other." And though "otherness" is currently a fashionable term among the literati, studies on Chicano culture have yet to attain the status of other worthy intellectual pursuits. This negligence toward a discourse of "the other," I claim, is a direct result of norms that confirm the inherent superiority of one set of values, representations, and discourse (ours = the subject) over another (theirs = the other). Indeed, human beings, as normative animals, are relentless creators of evaluative standards that serve to approve and disapprove of qualities, symbols, and actions. Naturally, those discourses closer to the "subject" (reflecting norms that are personal, familiar, or known) will be privileged over those of the "other," that is, normative values that are alien, unfamiliar, or unknown.

Like any other group, Chicanos respond at an in-group level to cultural change, and their satires and comedies represent finely tuned devices that register their assessment of conduct. Audiences thus react favorably or negatively to the texts or performances of comics and satirists because of their familiarity with specific normative paradigms encoded in cultural conventions. The interpretation of norms underlying satiric and comic discourse, therefore, involves neither reductionist nor Manichaean procedures. The observer who analyzes cultural expressions must decipher a complex interplay of evaluative possibilities that require abilities and qualities that are already familiar to literary scholars: knowledge of cultural traditions, theoretical soundness, ample reading, sensitivity to subtlety and nuance, and discernment of major trends. The hegemonic spectrum that I have suggested describes graphically some of the abstract and concrete norms and representations that have evolved in the Western tradition to condemn and praise positive and negative values. But satiric discourse is capable of adhering to an inexhaustible breadth of normative patterns expressed as cultural beliefs. In the history of Chicanos, for instance, there is a recognizable pattern of inherited evaluative paradigms that are adapted to changing sociocultural conditions.

The *pocho* and the *pachuco* are two figures that represent fundamental experiences in Chicano history: cultural contact with Anglo-Americans and urban adaptation. Both figures have antecedents in Mexican popular tradition and are inspired by models found throughout the Spanish heritage which, in turn, may ultimately be traced to similar figures in the Greco-Roman classical world. Often perceived as comic distortions of Mexican and Anglo-American cultural forms, the *pocho* and the *pachuco* have undergone a radical reinterpretation in the last twenty years. During this period a new generation of literary authors, reassessing important aspects of the Chicano experience, converted their previously stigmatized (humorous) characteristics into the qualities of figures that have attained dignified (epic) proportions. Through this endeavor the *pocho* and the *pachuco* figures underwent a reassessment; no longer treated comically as the *other*, they now adopted, satirically, the voice of the *subject*.

These generic findings suggest a number of theoretical and practical implications in other satiric and comic traditions and texts. In addition, a number of important older and younger Chicano satirists must be acknowledged and their works given the appropriate attention of literary scholars. Among the former are Julio G. Arce, Lalo Guerrero, La Chata Nolesca, "La Bella" Netti and Jesús Rodríguez, Daniel Venegas, and many others whose names or pseudonyms are known through anecdotes or are found in archives, in old newspapers, and in phonograph recordings. The work of contemporary satirists is yet to be undertaken; some of these are: José Antonio Burciaga, Margarita Cota-Cárdenas, Sergio Hernández, Cheech Marín, Marisela Norte, Javier Pacheco, Pablo Rodríguez, Gina Valdés, Alma Cervantes, and the groups known as "Con Safos," "Culture Clash," and "Latin Anonymous."

Although the present book has not been a comparative nor an exhaustive study of Valdez, Montoya, and Hinojosa, it is of interest to point out some significant similarities in their works. Thus, the complex problems implicit in recent urban adaptation and the influence of Anglo-American life are prominent in the writings of the three. While the themes of Chicano assimilation and acculturation had traditionally been portrayed comically by the *pocho* and the *pachuco* figures, the protagonists of these writers break with this pattern by demonstrating both their loyalty to traditional Mexican culture as well as the intention to overcome the new conditions posed by an Anglo-American world. These are newly conceived heroic models who display a number of significant Chicano virtues: competent bilingualism, familiarity with rural and urban cultures, and adherence to ethical principles that set them in opposition to powerful though corrupt community enemies. They are protagonists who have ceased to be treated comically and have entered into satiric discourse. Thus, Valdez, Montoya, and Hinojosa—each responding distinctively to their interpretation of the conflicts experienced by their created characters—deflect the satirical barbs away from community targets, redirecting them toward sources and agents that threaten the well-being of Chicanos. Such an endeavor would not have been possible without that artistic but powerful weapon that redefines normative paradigms: satire.

Notes

1. Satire: An Introduction

1. Some scholars distinguish between "satire" and the "satiric": the former as an artistic genre whose canonical texts form a tradition and the latter to include other types of discourse that employ techniques and attitudes of attack and that may properly be distinguished as a mode (Worcester 4).

2. Although principally discussing the novel, in his introductory chapter Petro presents a useful overview of some of the central issues on satire as a genre (1–23). See Van Rooy for a detailed history and usage of the term. For valuable modern views on Roman satire, see Coffey and Anderson. For recent work in the ever-expanding field of English satirical studies, see Rawson and Guilhamet. A brief but profitable discussion on the difficulties in defining satire is found in Elliot's "The Definition of Satire." Most of these works include valuable bibliographies.

3. According to the broad conception of satire, this is an open, metageneric convention whose origins can be traced to magic and ritual and which reflects the full range of human discourse—including canonical and noncanonical literary texts and a variety of popular and folkloric expressions—whose presence has survived in mimetic and nonmimetic forms into our day. An important species is that of Menippean or Varronian satire among whose many cultivators may be included such diverse authors as Lucian, Petronious, Apuleius, Chaucer, Rabelais, Swift, Erasmus, Voltaire, and Dostoyevski. In my approach to satire, I adhere to a Menippean conception.

For a comprehensive bibliography on Menippean satire, see Kirk, who includes many citations valuable to the study of satire in general. Influential views on the Menippean tradition are those of Frye (309) and Bakhtin (*Dostoevsky's Poetics* 133–147). For the Menippean tradition in Varro, Lucian, Seneca, and Erasmus, see Benda's doctoral dissertation; for Chaucer, see Payne; Nelson applies the tradition in studying the work of the contemporary Cuban writer Guillermo Cabrera Infante.

4. In this regard Rosenheim's "satiric spectrum" is particularly valuable. His precise definition is: "*satire consists of an attack by means of a manifest fiction upon discernible historic particulars.*" I adhere to Rosen-

heim's conceptualization, although employing the term *satiric discourse* to include all manifestations of satire, canonical and noncanonical, literary, oral, and ideographic.

5. These two extremes of abstractions are not intended to represent a *consensus gentium*. Geertz describes this term as "the notion that there are some things that all men will be found to agree upon as right, real, just, or attractive and that these things are, therefore, in fact right, real, just, or attractive" (38–39). I wish to argue that the notions here included (chaos, fear, and so forth) have wide cultural applications and only acquire meaning and significance within the context of specific cultural conventions.

6. Antinomies such as the ones I propose have been present since classical times and are represented, for instance, as soul and body, continuing into the present as idealism and materialism. Rhetoric developed from such an opposing approach whereby an orator debates a contender who argues between good and evil, truth and falseness, and so forth (Lloyd). I must insist, however, that my purpose here is only to suggest that certain abstract notions have a direct relationship to the creation and survival of stereotyped notions of normative and deviant values and, hence, that corresponding fictional figures have appeared to embody such notions. Invariably, and ironically, the discussion of such oppositional elements can itself be the subject of debate: see the variety of responses in the Norms in Satire Symposium held in 1964, where Frye poses the grotesque as a deviancy from the norm (9–10); and Petro's discussion on these responses (*Modern Satire* 17–21). Jameson, who cites Nietzsche and Derrida to support his view, mentions, among other figures, the barbarian, the woman, and the alien as archetypal figures of the other (114–115). Thus from a poststructuralist perspective, one may conceive that opposing principles stand as a deconstruction of normative values (and vice versa!).

7. The terms *subject* and *other* are undergoing close scrutiny in contemporary times; for valuable discussions on the origins, applications, and controversial debates on these terms, see Smith, Davis, Dallery, Habermas (*The Philosophical*), Stallybrass, and de Certeau.

8. Jameson describes this term (39); Raymond Williams provides a succinct description of its evolution (95–100).

9. It must be pointed out that the creation of the hero in modern times—a figure who sometimes adopts the roles and values customarily identified with marginality: delinquency, sin, madness, lechery, and so forth—is an apt reflection of the profound social and moral changes occurring today. This contemporary puzzle is also known as "postmodernism," a condition in which individuals find extreme difficulty in ascertaining the soundness of ethical choices. In the debates regarding this modern anxiety, there are suggestions ranging from total relativism to a return to the secure (normative) simplicity of yesterday, but it is unlikely that once normative categories are overturned the answer can satisfactorily be found in either futurism or anachronism, or else nihilism or authoritarianism. For a discussion of the difficulties encountered in this period, see the valuable essays

edited by Arac. Rosaura Sánchez ("Postmodernism") provides a most revealing analysis of this concept in relation to Chicano literature.

10. My thesis is that these figures emerge within the cultural parameters of a given group, and I do not, therefore, advocate a strict (unidimensional) reading of the authorial meaning in literary texts, as it may be suggested, for example, in Hirsch's hermeneutic approach. Indeed, satiric texts are frequently read literally until it is discovered that they offer an opposite meaning or an alternative cogent reading. Among many examples, one might mention *El libro de buen amor*, which has elicited different and conflicting interpretations that range from the view that the author, Juan Ruiz, was hypocritical and immoral or else virtuous and a defender of the Christian faith (Walker 231). Another pertinent example that might be considered as Menippean satire (Payne xi n. 3) is the *Lazarillo de Tormes*, whose protagonist's actions were once read as the biographical or the quasibiographical experiences of a naive author and, in modern times, as the corrupt testimony of a narrator who stands in sharp contrast with the ideological perspective of the author. The case of *Lazarillo* is particularly pertinent, since its textual ambiguities and our total ignorance of the author's social and historical orientation—and thus of his normative values—have allowed for disparate readings, even at a surface level.

11. Jameson mentions how opposing voices are marginalized, silenced, fragmented, or reappropriated by the hegemonic culture (85). For a discussion of the concept of hegemony in the work of Gramsci, see Bates.

12. The distinction I make is solely for illustrative purposes, since I argue that a hegemonic spectrum covers a wide range of normative values, rendering the borderline cases (i.e., those aligned with comedy and tragedy) especially difficult to interpret. This difficulty is further complicated because of the presence of irony in these genres. In this sense the "(satiric) hegemonic spectrum" is only one more modality of the bipartite conception of satire (ranging from the comic to the tragic) as it is practiced, for example, by Horace and Juvenal. I do insist, however, that it is in the normative area, hence grounded in historical and social values, that the reader must turn to interpret the tensions underlying satiric discourse. This is a substantial departure from strictly synchronic conceptions of satire, such as Frye's Mythos of Winter (*Anatomy* 223–239). Though favoring tragic over comic satire, Weber provides an insightful discussion of this problem.

13. When groups that have been defeated cease to pose a threat to the values of their opponents, they are likely to be represented in comic terms by the winners. For example, in the United States the figures of English aristocrats, Southerners, and Nazis at one time symbolized the norms of foes—respectively representing the enemies defeated militarily during the American Revolution, the Civil War, and World War II—but today they frequently are the subject of comic treatment in American popular culture. As it has been suggested above, an important aspect in the study of a culture during significant and conflictive periods is how these tensions are portrayed in comic and satirical figures.

14. The public sphere of satiric discourse may be said to have arisen in a "shame culture" in which normative behavior is guided by a code enforced by the collectivity, whereas in its opposite, or "guilt culture," individual conduct is internalized and thus represents a personal responsibility. The concept was convincingly applied to literary texts by Dodds, in *The Greeks and the Irrational*, who contrasts Homeric man's "enjoyment of *timé*, public esteem" (17) to the development of a sense of guilt whereby "sin is a condition of the will, a disease of man's inner consciousness" (36). The concept of guilt/shame as a cultural distinction has important implications in the development of satire, since an important aspect of its attack—whether serious or comic—relies on the public debasement of the satirized. (See Aguilar for an example from southern Mexico.) The shame-guilt dichotomy may help explain the appearance of a satiric spirit during periods and situations when public controversies intensify.

15. The reader ought to be aware that the term *Chicano* has diverse interpretations. Sometimes a restricted meaning is given (1) politically, to refer to individuals who identify with the political ideology arising during the 1960s; (2) culturally, alluding to individuals of Mexican ancestry but who are either unfamiliar or uncomfortable with Mexican cultural codes—a usage that differentiates them from "Mexicanos" or "Latinos"; (3) historically, an ample meaning that subsumes a wide variety of perspectives, that is, it refers to the full range of historical experiences of the people of Mexican descent living or having lived in the territories that are now considered the United States. This ample sense is the only one I employ throughout the present book.

16. In spite of its importance, to this date there have been few studies on Chicano satire. See García for a brief description of satire in the works of Luis Valdez; Fraire-Aldava for ironic and satiric tone and meaning in the essays of Octavio Romano. For Chicano humor see A. Paredes ("The Anglo-American" and "Folk Medicine"), Limón ("Agringado Joking"), Castro, Reyna, and Edmonson.

17. A newspaper published in El Paso, Texas, in 1892, referred to this group as "Ex-Mexicanos" or "Ex-Mexicans" ("Este Periódico"). This colonial population later underwent what Américo Paredes ("Folklore de los grupos") has described as an "inter cultural conflict" with Anglo-Americans.

18. There certainly had been numerous organizing efforts before the 1960s but as Acuña's *Occupied America* (64–69, 194–201, 309–312) demonstrates, these attempts did not achieve the interregional, transgenerational, and multicultural all-encompassing scope attained in the recent past. In his *A Texas-Mexican "Cancionero,"* Américo Paredes (27–28) argues persuasively that the contemporary assimilation of Chicanos into the American mainstream resulted from the success of the Chicano protest movement.

19. An early expression of this artistic consciousness was voiced by Luis Valdez ("El Teatro Campesino"). Three years later, in 1969, in *El Plan de Santa Barbara*, Chicano faculty and students urged institutional support for a Chicano curriculum that included courses on Chicano literature. Numer-

ous Chicano publications during this period welcomed the submission of creative works thus encouraging the efforts of new writers. Valuable sources for this early period are G. Rojas' "Chicano/Raza Bibliography," Leal's "Chicano Journals," Lomelí and Urioste's *Chicano Perspectives*, and Eger's *A Bibliography*.

20. Because this term has been frequently applied as a label to include a wide variety of Chicano perspectives, I employ it in the present work in this ample sense. The reader, nevertheless, ought to be aware of the more restricted meaning which it is often given: referring strictly to individuals who identify with the political consciousness arising during the 1960s. See note 15.

21. Although it is doubtful that Rodriguez was influenced by Robles, his autobiographic *Hunger*, ironically, has some dramatic resemblances with *Los desarraigados*. For example, in a final scene at his parental house one Christmas evening, Rodriguez describes his father as a figure culturally dispossessed and alienated from his children, in a manner that reminds the reader of the denouement at the end of Robles' play as the protagonist muses on his lost children and the nostalgia he feels for his homeland. Thus, although recounted from opposing perspectives, *Hunger* and *Los desarraigados* interface at important thematic and ideological levels.

22. On the one hand, *Hunger* is widely read in American educational institutions, and its author, an admitted academic drop-out, is hailed as an authority on a variety of Chicano issues. Ramón Saldívar ("Ideologies" 26) has mentioned how in a few years Rodriguez' book, and views, have received wide dissemination. The play *Los desarraigados*, on the other hand, won a distinguished national prize in Mexico (Premio "El Nacional" 1955) and its first performance was attended by members of the Mexican cultural and political elite (Robles 11). Raymond Paredes ("Autobiography") provides an insightful discussion on Rodriguez' indebtedness to the American tradition of conversion whereby a literary or historical character undergoes a profound moral or spiritual transformation.

23. The scarce or else distorted view on Chicanos in the literature before the 1960s is pointed out, among others, by Romano, Padilla, A. Paredes ("On Ethnographic Work"), and Rosaldo. One of the important contributions of Gamio's work in his research on Mexican immigration in the United States was his recruitment and training of Chicano assistants who helped prepare, conduct, and summarize field interviews (*Mexican Immigration* vii). Chicanos, nevertheless, have always shown interest in the events occurring outside of their communities. A cursory reading of Spanish-language newspapers in the United States, for example, demonstrates that at every period in their history Chicanos have maintained deep interest in all aspects of worldwide cultural and political life. For a brief overview of Chicano journalism see Ríos and Castillo, and F. Gutierrez. The role of Chicano newspapers in the promotion of literature is the subject of Stefano's doctoral dissertation.

24. A general overview of this problem can be found in McWilliams' *North from Mexico*. Robinson's *With the Ears of Strangers* includes abundant examples of the negative image of Mexicans as literary figures. The

attitude is also amply documented in De León's *They Called Them Greasers*. For a Mexican assessment of this perspective, see Ortega y Medina, *México en la conciencia anglosajona*.

25. Gumperz and Hernández-Chávez suggest this relationship between an in-group and out-group frame of reference when discussing Spanish-English code switching. This linguistic trend, however, has begun to change, especially in the last twenty or thirty years, when English monolingualism has become relatively common among Chicanos. For a valuable assessment of the esoteric-exoteric factor in Chicano folklore, see A. Paredes, "On Ethnographic Work".

26. A useful overview of the various historical currents may be seen in Cortés' entry for "Mexicans" in the *Harvard Encyclopedia of American Ethnic Groups*. For another view on distinctions among Chicanos as reflected in their folkore, see A. Paredes, "El folklore." A number of critics have discussed the various cultural currents informing literary works, see Ortego's "Chicano Renaissance," Leal's "Mexican American Literature," R. Paredes' "Evolution of Chicano Literature," Ybarra-Frausto's "Chicano Movement," and Hernández' "On the Theoretical" and "El Mexico."

27. The *pocho* as an agent of Anglo-American values, however, may also be the object of scorn on the part of Chicanos; examples of this attitude can be seen in Limón ("Agringado Joking") and A. Paredes ("Folk Medicine"). It is obvious that the attack on the Margaritas also reflects an antifeminine tradition. The Judeo-Christian background of Spanish misogyny is discussed by Cantarino. For views on women in Spanish and Latin American literature, see Miller's anthology. For the response of Chicanas to stereotypes, see Herrera-Sobek.

28. For a thorough study of the antecedents in antiquity of this urban contempt for rustic traits, see Ramage's *"Urbanitas"*. The attitude that the culture of the learned is the only one worthy of aesthetic enjoyment, whereas that of rural populations is deplorable may be seen in one of the first literary commentaries in the Spanish Middle Ages: the Marqués de Santillana in his "Proemio al condestable de Portugal"; this view is also evident in the depiction of mountain girls as comic savages in the *serrana* episodes of Ruiz' *Libro de buen amor*. Influential Renaissance authors such as the anonymous writer of *Lazarillo de Tormes* and Cervantes in his *Don Quijote* will depict the *villano* as an uncouth and comic figure. In his seminal study of the ballads sung by blind minstrels in Spain, Caro Baroja (164–171) mentions the depictions of such deviant humorous figures. These figures were subjected to ridicule in a variety of genres from the seventeenth through the nineteenth centuries.

29. See a study of similar urban figures in Leal's "Pícaros and léperos."

30. The practice of mixing languages and dialects is known as heteroglossia or code switching and has produced a large bibliography. It is a common phenomenon that occurs in communities that employ several linguistic norms, although it is a usage generally condemned when considered as a menace to linguistic homogeneity. Now dated but still valuable in this field

is Hernández-Chávez, Cohen, and Beltrano and Teschmer et al. A recent (1982) compilation of articles is that of Amastae and Elías-Olivares.

31. See A. Jiménez for a recompilation of this type of improvisation (*Nueva picardía mexicana* 83–93).

32. Villalongín's manuscript uses the title "Chin Chun Chan" at the heading of this dialogue. For a brief description of this popular zarzuela—represented hundreds, perhaps thousands of times—see Reyes de la Maza (*Circo* 340). Américo Paredes includes a variant from "Chin Chun Chan" collected from oral sources, evidently a border adaptation (*Cancionero* 165–166). Two lines from the zarzuela read "Como el yanqui nos invade / el Inglés hay que aprender"; this is collected by Paredes as "Como estamos en Texas / el Inglés hay que aprender." Paredes' variant is of great importance, since it demonstrates how Mexican cultural forms underwent changes when represented before Chicano audiences.

33. In the nationalist fervor triggered by the Mexican Revolution, there appeared attempts to reverse this trend employing Mestizo and Indian figures in normative roles. The most notable efforts in this respect were led by the three Mexican muralists Diego Rivera, David Alfaro Siqueiros, and José Clemente Orozco. In many other fields, Mexican artists and thinkers have been engaged in this reassessment away from a Eurocentric conception of Mexican culture to one based on native perspectives.

34. There is a *corrido* of a horse named "El Pochi" (Acosta 75); a reference to the "pochis de California" (Campa, *Spanish Folk-Poetry* 214); and a rancho del "pochi" near the border of Sinaloa and Chihuahua. See Villanueva and Santamaría for additional examples of the word.

35. See Chacón, "The Chicano Immigrant Press in Los Angeles" and Gonzales, "Forgotten Pages."

36. I wish to thank Federico Sánchez for pointing out this usage.

37. José Vasconcelos' testimony indicates how the term *pochismo* was used around 1913: "Palabra que se usa en California para designar al descastado que niega de lo mexicano aunque lo tiene en la sangre y procura ajustar todos sus actos al mimetismo de los amos actuales de la región" (Word used in California to designate someone disloyal to his own kind and who rejects his Mexicanness, although carrying it in the blood, and who tries to adjust all his acts to the imitations of the present masters of the region). It is significant that Vasconcelos also applies the term in conjunction with certain Mexican political figures—Santa Anna, Juárez, Díaz, Calles, and so forth—whom he accuses of being tools of American economic and cultural expansionism.

38. The word *Chicano* became widely used after the undergraduates at the University of California, Berkeley, chose the name MECHA (Movimiento Estudiantil Chicano de Aztlán) for their organization. One of the leaders of this group, Manuel Delgado, suggested that the word *pocho* was equivalent to *Chicano*. Macías also makes this claim. The "Minutes of MASC-MECHA" at the University of California, Berkeley, by Lenny Villagómez (presently unlocated) would help shed considerable information on

the creation of the student organization MECHA (Movimiento Estudiantil Chicano de Aztlán), as well as the ideological reasons and the context in which the term *Chicano* was adopted in contemporary times.

39. Richard Rodriguez, a student at the University of California, Berkeley, rediscovered *Pocho* in the late 1960s and recommended it to Octavio Romano who quoted from it in the journal *El Grito* ("The Historical and Intellectual" 33). Villarreal's novel, which had been out of print, was published again and is now considered a classic of Chicano literature and is reprinted regularly.

40. The term is used as a nickname for an inhabitant of El Paso, Texas: evolving from *Paso*, to *pacho*, and *pachuco*, or *chuco*. Originally the term seems to have had a strict local identification as can be seen in the usage of the term in the traditional ballad "Raymundo 'El pachuco,'" lacking any reference to either urban settings, *caló*, or zoot suits.

41. In Mexico this figure appeared around the 1940s; they soon came to be known as *tarzanes* because of their long hair and in a parody of the popular Hollywood figure by that name. A comparison between *tarzanes* and *pachucos* appears in Hernández, *Canciones* (59–65).

42. These names—*pisaverdes, currutacos, mequetrefes, dandys, petimetres, catrines,* and *rotos*—were employed to describe individuals with an exaggerated attachment to fashionable clothing. Many of these figures were too poor or too unsophisticated to maintain an elegant life-style. In 1799 Manuel Gómez Marín published a satirical poem on the figure of the *currutaco:* "El currutaco por alambique." The original manuscript is in the Biblioteca Nacional de México and has been edited by Marcela Uribe Hernández.

43. For a most valuable overview of this phenomenon, see Moers *The Dandy.* The influence of this figure on France is evident in *El dandismo,* an anthology that includes impressions by Balzac, Baudelaire, and Barbey d'Aurevilly.

44. The image of the poorly dressed individual—who leads a hand-to-mouth existence—has deep roots in the Spanish and Mediterranean literary traditions. It may suffice to mention, among many other texts, the old clothes and permanent hunger of the squire in *Lazarillo de Tormes* (1554), whose example will be followed by Lazarillo himself; the dispute in the medieval dialogue "Elena y María" (ca. 1280), where the hunger of the clergyman and the poor clothing of the courtier are subjected to ridicule; the constant pleading by the great Hispano-Arabic poet, Ibn Quzman (died ca. 1160), for his patrons to remedy his comic dress and his persistent hunger; and the playful begging by the wandering students known as *goliards,* requesting food and clothing.

45. Chicanos have been drawn to adopt many of the fashions and lifestyles of the United States and, in doing so, have been portrayed comically. In the novel *Las aventuras de don Chipote* by Daniel Venegas, published in 1928, the protagonist arrives in Los Angeles and soon trades his rural attire for the clothing that is fashionable in the city. In his depiction of Don Chi-

pote, Venegas ridicules his awkward new taste (118). The flappers and their unconventional way of life are mentioned in the song "El ferrocarrilero," recorded during the 1920s. A similar comical depiction is evident in a song recorded during the 1960s or "hippie" era, "Felipe, el jipi."

46. The adoption of the business suit marks a major adaptation to urban norms on the part of traditional immigrant folk. See a Spanish-language newspaper advertisement for suits, available on credit, in Hernández, *Canciones* 23.

47. In the eastern United States, the "zoot suiter" was frequently associated with blacks; Mazón (7) mentions that the origins of the suit may be traced to Harlem or London where those who wore it were known as "spivs" or "wide boys." José Montoya remembers one of his elders mentioning that Chicanos became *pachucos* after borrowing the Filipino style of clothes (personal communication, 8 February 1987).

48. The loss of the Mexican territories and its impact on the Mexican national consciousness is the subject of a chapter, "El trauma del 47," in Jorge Carrión's *Mito* (22–37).

49. See a display of criticism toward *pachucos* by traditional Mexican rural folk in A. Paredes (*With His Pistol* 34). The aspirations of the returning Chicano veterans of World War II were antithetical to the *pachuco* life-style as can be seen in Morin's recounting in *Among the Valiant.* See Endore for the case on behalf of the zoot suiters accused of the Sleepy Lagoon incident as presented by their defense committee.

50. For an overview of the antecedents of the term *pocho* in Mexican literature, see Leal ("Mexican American Literature") and Vasconcelos. Madrid-Barela ("Pochos") gives examples of how the term is used by some contemporary Chicano authors.

51. An overview of the reaction toward *pachucos* on the part of the authorities in Los Angeles can be seen in McWillians (227–258) and Acuña (323–329). G. Sánchez and Adler provide an early assessment on the *pachuco* phenomena as caused by social and historical conditions. See contemporary views of the *pachuco* as a symbolic and historic figure in Grajeda, Madrid-Barela ("In Search"), and Flores ("La dualidad del pachuco"); for a psychological approach to the (mis)treatment of *pachucos*, see Mazón.

52. There are few testimonies of the point of view of *pachucos* regarding their life-style. The poets José Montoya, in "El Louie," and Raúl Salinas, in "Homenaje al pachuco" have sought to recreate this perspective.

2. Luis Valdez and *Actos* of Teatro Campesino

1. In my transcriptions from the *Actos*, I have standardized the spelling, thus avoiding repetitive notations regarding the irregularities found in the original.

2. For an account of the playwright's early farmworking years, theatrical and political interests, and initial involvement in the strike, see the interview "Platicando con Luis Valdez" by Morton. For the beginnings of Teatro

Campesino, see the interviews conducted by Bagby. The origins, themes, techniques, and the mixing of politics and art in the San Francisco Mime Troupe are discussed by its founder, Ronnie Davis, in an interview by Ragué Arias.

3. Duckworth (236–271) discusses a variety of comic roles in Roman plays. For a contrast between the frivolity represented by city folk and the superior morality prevalent in the country, see Hunter (109–113). Bieber (109–113) includes illustrations of parasite figures. The relationship between masters and servants is discussed by Segal. Welsford traces the evolution of the figure of the fool. See Grismer for the introduction of Plautine characters into Spain.

4. My colleague Gerardo Luzuriaga suggests the *pasos* of the Spanish playwright Lope de Rueda as a source of inspiration for the *actos* of Valdez. This is a possibility that ought to be investigated, since (1) de Rueda's short representations are similar to the *actos* of Teatro Campesino and (2) the Mime Troupe—an early influence on Valdez—has represented some of the Spaniard's works.

5. Picaresque figures are perceived from the perspective of an outsider-narrator who claims to have succeeded in becoming an insider—as Lazarillo's running commentary, in *Lazarillo de Tormes*, traces his ascent to a privileged position (Guillén 83). The viewpoint of the picaro, however, is in turn assessed from the system of values held by an omniscient author who, as an insider, shares the reader's skepticism regarding the questionable success claimed by the narrator.

6. A similar exchange of roles appears in the play *El delantal blanco* by the Chilean playwright Sergio Vodanovic. For a discussion of the significance of the mask in Valdez' work, see Fabre.

7. Griffin describes how the ending of satires represents a difficult artistic problem.

8. This move to El Rey made Teatro Campesino totally independent from UFWOC. The company was then established as El Centro Campesino Cultural, a not-for-profit organization. Two years later, in 1969, the company moved again, to Fresno, California. These changes of location are briefly described by Valdez in "History of the Teatro Campesino."

9. The pronunciation "Reagen" is a mocking allusion to Ronald Reagan, then governor of California (who insisted on the latter pronunciation of his name) and an opponent of the unionizing efforts of the farmworkers.

10. Although the figure of the Mexican-American has often been identified with the *pocho*, by the 1960s the latter term had acquired such negative connotations that most Chicano writers avoided its usage. It is possible that Chicano youths strongly influenced by Anglo-American culture would have been offended had the Teatro utilized the term *pocho*.

11. Huerta (66) has noted how the ending of this *acto* was significantly altered in its videotaped version: "[in it] the operation was masterminded by a soft-spoken scientist (played by Valdez) whose models do go with their buyers and who are being placed in every major center of MeChicano popu-

lation. One day soon, these 'Mexican-Americans' will become Chicanos and defend the rights of their people rather than fight against them."

12. Santamaría (959) records this word as a meaning applied to a sheep or ram of any age or to a deceived husband. This connotation is, undoubtedly, related to that of *cornudo* or *cabrón* (cuckold) and so derived from the association with the horns of the animal. Among Chicanos, however, this usage has become proverbial in referring to the lover of an unfaithful (generally married) woman. Also Sánchez, and Sancha in Galván (106).

13. Valdez remembers how the frequent use of the word *vendido* (sellout) among Chicano groups during the 1960s originated the idea of creating an *acto* with a number of Chicano characters who would literally "sell out" (Hernández "Interview with Luis Valdez").

14. Undoubtedly an important influence on the criticism that Chicanos have of U.S. education has been the contrast with the educational gains made in Mexico since the revolution. In spite of the small budgets of their schools, the postrevolutionary orientation of Mexican teachers has emphasized mass education and social equality. The quality and treatment many Chicanos received from Mexican teachers is often superior to the attitudes they later encounter from U.S. educators. Thus, the children of immigrant parents oftentimes first meet in American classrooms and from American teachers the effects of racial and cultural discrimination. It is an area deserving of ample study.

15. The list of works in Chicano literature where childhood and adolescence is portrayed would be extensive. A few of the contemporary texts including this theme are José Antonio Villarreal's novel *Pocho*, Rolando Hinojosa's *KCDTS*, Rudy Anaya's *Bless Me, Ultima*, and Margarita Cota-Cárdenas in *Puppet*; the autobiographies of Ernesto Galarza, *Barrio Boy*, and Richard Rodriguez' *Hunger of Memory*; and the poetic work of Bernice Zamora in *Restless Serpents* and of Gina Valdés in *Comiendo lumbre*. Many periodicals have focused on this area, such as *Con Safos Magazine* during the late 1960s and *Lowrider Magazine* in the 1970s. This is another area, virtually unexplored in Chicano literature, that needs special attention.

16. The stage directions for the scene at college do not ask for a white mask for the professor. Since the negative characterization had already been made by the elementary and high school teachers, the mask device is no longer necessary.

17. For an example of the problems involved in performing before foreign audiences, see the many explanatory notes accompanying Valdez' article "Teatro di mutamento," in the Italian theatrical magazine *Sipario*.

18. For some of the experiences encountered by Chicanos in the military service, see Morin (67–74), Hernández, *Canciones* (67–71), Vera, Guzmán, and Trujillo.

19. See a partial list of these groups in F. Jiménez' "Dramatic Principles" (109–111) and Huerta's *Chicano Theater* (273).

20. Hernández, "Interview with Luis Valdez." Frischmann points out

how the *mito* also involves a critical position, although from a higher moral plane.

21. For a view of the changes undergone by Valdez and the Teatro during this period, see Morton's "La Serpiente."

22. See Bagby's interview with Luis Valdez for a description of the problems involved in the creation of Teatro Campesino. Critical perspectives on the change from a farmworkers' theater to religious or commercial productions and the implications for Chicanos are those of Fuentes, Kanellos, and Yarbro-Bejarano; Yarbro-Bejarano cites the critical reactions to Valdez's *mito* on the part of the Latin American playwrights Enrique Buenaventura and Augusto Boal.

23. Balkan discusses briefly the marketing complexities involved in the promotion of the film *Zoot Suit*.

3. José Montoya: From the RCAF to the Trio Casindio

1. Montoya's vocation as a visual artist has continued to the present: he is an active painter and is professor of art at California State University, Sacramento. Peschel-Tentsch provides a detailed description of Montoya's life as well as the poet's views on art and literature. See also Bruce Novoa's *Chicano Authors* (115–136)

2. Montoya is preparing to publish a comprehensive collection of his poetry: *In Formation*. For many years Montoya read poetry under the sponsorship of an art collective in Sacramento known as the Royal Chicano Air Force (RCAF). The group adopted this name after someone noted that its original choice—Rebel Chicano Art Front—was also the acronym of the Royal Canadian Air Force. Keeping with the irony of the situation, they decided to become the air command of the Chicano nation and renamed themselves as the Royal Chicano Air Force. The group would use military titles and terminology and, as a leading member of this group of art activists, Montoya is often addressed by his peers as "General."

3. In recent years Montoya has added songwriting to his poetic production. Thus far he has published one phonographic album—*Trio Casindio and the Royal Chicano Air Force*—with many of his compositions. He sings the lead voice for Trio Casindio, a group that performs principally before Chicano audiences. Castellano, Lint, and Bruce-Novoa (*Chicano Authors* 14–25) have analyzed specific poems of Montoya.

4. This is part of a widespread tradition, see Amades. See Stewart for a thorough discussion of this subgenre.

5. Montoya (Hernández "Interview with Montoya") said he was inspired by the parody on Cervantes' Don Quijote made by the comic "Tin Tan" in a film *(Un Quijote sin mancha!)*.

6. Given the pervasive Roman Catholicism among Chicanos, were there efforts to recruit them for the priesthood? There is ample need for studies regarding the role of the Roman Catholic church in the Chicano community.

7. The Brown Berets were barrio-based groups of young people organized during the 1960s, formed as social and political advocates for community

well-being. They were modeled on the Black Panthers but did not attain the national prominence of this black organization.

8. The term *Lulac* refers to the League of United Latin American Citizens, an organization formed by Chicanos in 1929 and still widely active.

9. Jacobson (249) concludes that most reasons for code switching are socially conditioned. In "Spanish Codes" Rosaura Sánchez mentions some important peer group considerations in the code switches found among Chicanos.

4. Rolando Hinojosa: Klail City Death Trip Series

1. The name *Klail City Death Trip Series* was suggested to Hinojosa by Lesy's book *Wisconsin Death Trip*, organized as a collage of texts and pictures re-creating local life (personal communication 7 July 1985). The parallels with Lesy's text are also evident in the explanatory subtitle of *The Valley: A Re-creation in Narrative Prose of a Portfolio of Etchings, Engravings, Sketches, and Silhouettes by Various Artists in Various Styles, Plus a Set of Photographs from a Family Album.*

2. The individual volumes were written in the following order:

1. *Estampas del valle y otras obras: EV*
2. *Klail City y sus alrededores: KC*
3. *Korean Love Songs: KLS*
4. *Claros varones de Belken: CVB*
5. *Mi querido Rafa: MQR*
6. *Rites and Witnesses: RW*
7. *Partners in Crime: PC*

Although *Korean Love Songs* is a book of poems, it refers to events and characters that pertain to the overall narrative in the *KCDTS*. A new novel, *Becky and Her Friends*, published by Arte Publico Press, 1989, arrived too late to incorporate it in this discussion of Hinojosa's work.

3. Gonzales-Berry points out how Hinojosa adapted *costumbrismo* to his own historical, literary, and oral purposes in *Estampas del valle*. See Flores' discussion on some important narrative strategies employed by Hinojosa in *Rites and Witnesses*.

4. Hereafter, I shall refer to the individual volumes by their initials. For my present purposes, I quote from the Spanish orginal editions; the English translations are my own. I have refrained from using Hinojosa's translations because he frequently introduces emendations in the English renditions of his work; these changes made by the author on his texts and translations merit study. Hinojosa gives an idea of the painstaking editorial corrections he makes on his original manuscripts in his essays "Crossing the Line" (Saldivar, *Hinojosa Reader* 25–43) and "Writing Is Not a Process." The concept of "public sphere" is treated by Habermas *(Historia)*, and Hohendahl discusses the evolution and debates surrounding this concept.

5. Hinojosa discusses his firm historical and cultural roots in "The

Sense of Place" and "A Voice of One's Own." For a background on Hinojosa, see Bruce-Novoa, *Chicano Authors*.

6. Calderón has drawn parallels between Hinojosa and the chronicles of the Spanish medieval author Fernán Pérez de Guzmán, including the title *Generaciones y semblanzas* for the bilingual (U.S.) edition of *Klail City y sus alrededores*. Hinojosa also alludes to the Bible, Shakespeare, Dostoevski, Cervantes, *La Celestina*, and Matthew Arnold, among many others. It appears, however, that Hinojosa does not draw from a single literary source, nor does he adapt materials directly: the sources employed in the *KCDTS* seem to be points of departure that the author uses for his own aesthetic purposes. An illustration of this liberal use of sources is the column "De la vida real (en broma)"—appearing in numerous Texan newspapers during 1928–1965—by the local writer José Díaz. Hinojosa acknowledges Díaz as an author who had an early and deep influence on him and includes Díaz as one of his narrators, under the pseudonym P. Galindo (personal communication 7 July 1985). A similar argument may be made in regard to Lesy's *Wisconsin Death Trip*, a work mentioned by Hinojosa as an inspiration for naming the *KCDTS* (see n. 1). This is an area meriting further study based on interviews with the author as well as textual analyses of his work.

7. Oral transmitters frequently dispense with fundamental contextual data, assuming that the listener has sufficient information to interpret the recited text. In contrast, literary authors maintain a relative external autonomy and internal cogency in their works. Lord suggests this difference in his study of Homer: "To the [oral] audience the meaning of the theme involves its own experience of it as well. The communication of this supra-meaning is possible because of the community of experience of poet and audience. At our distance of time and space we can approach an understanding of the supra-meaning only by steeping ourselves in as much material in traditional poetry or in a given tradition as is available" (148). For a valuable and recent overview of oral studies, see Foley.

8. Does Hinojosa intend to achieve a parallel with Melville's *Moby Dick*? It seems perhaps far-fetched to compare the life of Jehú and the obsession of Captain Ahab in his pursuit of the white whale as it becomes a symbol of madness resulting from man's unbridled quest for the absolute. Yet in *Mi querido Rafa*, Jehú does reveal a silent but spirited struggle to survive the corrupt and absolute rule of the Klail-Cook-Blanchard family.

9. Ramón Saldívar has suggested the relevance of the "Corrido de Gregorio Cortez" in Hinojosa's *Korean Love Songs*. The influence of this ballad on Rafa Buenrostro is, undoubtedly, also a central motif throughout the *Klail City Death Trip Series*.

10. The Cook-Blanchard establishment is often alluded to as the "ranch" in the *KCDT* series, in what appears as a thinly veiled reference to the King Ranch. Its role in the eyes of the Chicanos from South Texas is described explicitly by Américo Paredes: "The official Texas Rangers are known as the *rinches de la Kineña* or Rangers of King Ranch, in accordance with the Borderer's belief that the Rangers were the personal strong-arm men of Richard King and the other cattle barons" (*With His Pistol* 24).

11. See J. A. Gutiérrez' parallel satirical description of the elaborate tactics used by Anglo-Americans to deprive Chicanos of their social, political, and economic rights.

12. Throughout the *KCDTS* numerous relationships between Anglo men and Chicanas are mentioned. For example, Becky Escobar's mother married a Caldwell; Viola Barragán marries a German national and, later, Guillete. Viola also has a relationship with Noddy Perkins. Duke dos Santos and de la Fuente suggest that Viola and Olivia San Esteban represent the New Hispanic women in the Americas.

13. Hinojosa's initial plans for *MQR* were to have Jehú address an imaginary listener in the manner of picaresque protagonist-narrators "Yo, señor . . ." (I, sir . . .) (personal communication, 23 November 1985)

14. In "Toward a Definition of the Picaresque," Guillén proposes the term *stricto sensu* (85) to refer to a tradition closely aligned to Spanish Renaissance models and *sensu lato* (93) for a wider definition of the term picaresque. See Bjornson for this latter usage in European fiction.

15. In *Partners in Crime*, Hinojosa has moved away from satire and into an epic. His newly announced volume in the *KCDTS*, *Becky and Her Friends*, is a promising satiric title.

Works Consulted

Acosta, Vicente S. "Some Surviving Elements of Spanish Folklore in Arizona." M.A. thesis, University of Arizona, 1951.

Acuña, Rodolfo. *Occupied America: A History of Chicanos*. 2d ed. New York: Harper and Row, 1981.

Aden, John M. "Towards a Uniform Satiric Terminology." *Satire Newsletter* 1 (1963–64): 30–32.

Adler, Patricia Rae. "The 1943 Zoot-Suit Riots: Brief Episode in a Long Conflict." In *An Awakening Minority: The Mexican-Americans*, ed. Manuel P. Servín, 142–158. 2d ed. Beverly Hills: Glencoe Press, 1974.

Aguilar, John L. "Shame, Acculturation, and Ethnic Relations." *Journal of Psychoanalytic Anthropology* 5.2 (1982): 156–171.

Amades, Juan. "El habla sin significado y la poesía popular disparatada." *Revista de Dialectología y Tradiciones Populares*. 15 (1959): 274–291.

Amastae, Jon, and Lucía Elías-Olivares, eds. *Spanish in the United States: Sociolinguistic Aspects*. Cambridge: Cambridge University Press, 1982.

Anaya, Rudolfo A. *Bless Me, Ultima*. Berkeley: Quinto Sol, 1972.

Anderson, William S. *Essays on Roman Satire*. Princeton: Princeton University Press, 1982.

Arac, Jonathan, ed. *Postmodernism and Politics*. Theory and History of Literature 28. Minneapolis: University of Minnesota Press, 1987.

Azuela, Mariano. *Los de abajo: Novela (cuadros y escenas de la revoluciones mexicanas)*. El Paso: El Paso del Norte, 1916.

Baca, Elfego. Cited in the editorial: "Los Mexicanos están en México." *La Estrella* (Las Cruces, N.M.), 1 November 1913, 1.

Bagby, Beth. "El Teatro Campesino: Interviews with Luis Valdez." *Tulane Drama Review* 4.11 (1967): 70–80.

Bakhtin, Mikhail. *Problems of Dostoevsky's Poetics*. Ed. and trans. Caryl Emerson. Theory and History of Literature 8. Minneapolis: University of Minnesota Press, 1984.

———. *Rabelais and His World*. Bloomington: Indiana University Press, 1984.

Balkan, D. Carlos. "From the *Carpa* to the Cinerama Drome: The Marketing of *Zoot Suit*." *Hispanic Business* 3.4 (1981): 10–11.

Balzac, Baudelaire, and Barbey d'Aurevilly. *El dandismo.* Trans. Joan Giner. Barcelona: Editorial Anagrama, 1974.

Barker, George C. "Pachuco: An American-Spanish Argot and Its Social Function in Tucson, Arizona." In *El Lenguaje de los Chicanos: Regional and Social Characteristics Used by Mexican Americans,* ed. Eduardo Hernández-Chávez et al., 183–201. Arlington, Va.: Center for Applied Linguistics, 1975.

Bates, Thomas R. "Gramsci and the Theory of Hegemony." *Journal of the History of Ideas* 36 (1975): 351–366.

Benda, Frederick Joseph. "The Tradition of Menippean Satire in Varro, Lucian, Seneca, and Erasmus." Ph.D. diss., University of Texas at Austin, 1979. University Microfilms International 7920085.

Bieber, Margaret. *The History of the Greek and Roman Theater.* Princeton: Princeton University Press, 1971.

Binder, Wolfgang. "José Montoya." *Erlangen Studien* 65.1 (1985): 117–135.

Bjornson, Richard. *The Picaresque Hero in European Fiction.* Madison: University of Wisconsin Press, 1977.

Blom, Jan Peter, and John Gumperz. "Social Meaning in Linguistic Structures: Code-switching in Northern Norway." In *Directions in Sociolinguistics,* ed. John J. Gumperz and Dell Hymes. New York: Holt, Rinehart and Winston, 1970.

Bocock, Robert. *Hegemony.* New York: Tavistock/Methuen, 1986.

Broyles, Yolanda Julia. "Hinojosa's *Klail City y sus alrededores:* Oral Culture and Print Culture." In Saldívar, *Hinojosa Reader* 109–132.

Bruce-Novoa, Juan. *Chicano Authors: Inquiry by Interview.* Austin: University of Texas Press, 1980.

———. *Chicano Poetry: A Response to Chaos.* Austin: University of Texas Press, 1982.

Calderón, Héctor. "On the Uses of Chronicle, Biography, and Sketch in Rolando Hinojosa's *Generaciones y semblanzas.*" In Saldívar, *Hinojosa Reader* 133–142.

Campa, Arthur L. *Spanish Folk-Poetry in New Mexico.* Albuquerque: University of New Mexico Press, 1946.

Campbell, Joseph. *The Hero with a Thousand Faces.* Bollingen Series 17. Princeton: Princeton University Press, 1973.

Cantarino, Vicente. "El antifeminismo y sus formas en la literatura medieval castellana." In *Homenaje a don Agapito Rey,* ed. Josep Roca-Pons, 93–116. Bloomington: Department of Spanish and Portuguese, Indiana University, 1980.

Caro Baroja, Julio. *Ensayo sobre la literatura de cordel.* Madrid: Revista de Occidente, 1969.

Carrillo, Leo. *The California I Love.* Englewood Cliffs, N.J. Prentice-Hall, 1961.

Carrión, Jorge. *Mito y magia del mexicano.* 1952. Mexico City: Editorial Nuestro Tiempo, 1970.

Castellano, Olivia. "José Montoya: Visions of Madness on the Open Road to the Temples of the Sun." *De Colores: Journal of Chicano Expression and Thought* 5.1–2 (1980): 82–92.

Castro, Rafaela. "Mexican Women's Sexual Jokes." *Aztlán: International Journal of Chicano Studies Research* 13.1–2 (1982): 275–293.

Certeau, Michel de. *Heterologies: Discourse on the Other.* Trans. Brian Massumi. Theory and History of Literature 17. Minneapolis: University of Minnesota Press, 1985.

Chacón, Ramón D. "The Chicano Immigrant Press in Los Angeles: The Case of 'El Heraldo de Mexico,' 1916–1920." *Journalism History* 4.2 (1977): 48+.

Chicano Coordinating Council for Higher Education. *El Plan de Santa Barbara: A Chicano Plan for Higher Education.* Oakland: La Causa Publications, 1969.

Coffey, Michael. *Roman Satire.* London: Methuen, 1976.

Cortés Carlos E. "Mexicans." *Harvard Encyclopedia of American Ethnic Groups,* ed. Stephan Thernstrom et al., 697–719. Cambridge: Mass.: Harvard University Press, 1980.

Cota-Cárdenas, Margarita. *Puppet.* Austin: Relampago Books, 1985.

Dallery, Arleen B., and Charles E. Scott. *The Question of the Other: Essays in Contemporary Continental Philosophy.* Albany: State University of New York Press, 1989.

Davis, Walter A. *Inwardness and Existence: Subjectivity in/and Hegel, Heidegger, Marx, and Freud.* Madison: University of Wisconsin Press, 1989.

De León, Arnoldo. *They Called Them Greasers: Anglo Attitudes toward Mexicans in Texas, 1821–1900.* Austin: University of Texas Press, 1983.

Díaz, José (P. Galindo). *De la vida real (en broma).* Mercedes, Tex.: N.p., 1965.

Dodds, E. R. *The Greeks and the Irrational.* Berkeley: University of California Press, 1973.

Duckworth, George E. *The Nature of Roman Comedy: A Study of Popular Entertainment.* Princeton: Princeton University Press, 1971.

Duke dos Santos, Mara I., and Patricia de la Fuente. "The Elliptic Female Presence as Unifying Force in the Novels of Rolando Hinojosa." In Saldívar, *Hinojosa Reader* 64–75.

Edmonson, Munro S. "Los Manitos: Patterns of Humor in Relation to Cultural Values." Ph.D. diss., Harvard University, 1952.

Eger, Ernestina N. *A Bibliography of Criticism of Contemporary Chicano Literature.* Berkeley: Chicano Studies Library Publications, 1982.

Elliott, Robert C. "The Definition of Satire: A Note on Method." *Yearbook of Comparative and General Literature* 11 (1962): 19–23.

———. "Satire." *The New Encyclopaedia Britannica: Macropaedia.* 15th ed. 1985. 23:182–185.

Endore, Guy. *The Sleepy Lagoon Mystery.* Los Angeles: Sleepy Lagoon Defense Committee, 1944.

Escudero, Carlos R. "El 'zoot suit' es pesadilla de sastre." *La Prensa* (San Antonio) 12 June 1943: 1+.

"Este Periódico. Sus trabajos, Editorial." *El Ciudadano* (El Paso), 12 March 1892, 1.

Fabre, Geneviève. "Dialectics of the Masks in el Teatro Campesino: From Images to Ritualized Events." *In Missions in Conflict: Essays on U.S.-Mexican Relations and Chicano Culture,* ed. Renate von Bardeleben, 93–99. Tübingen: Gunter Narr Verlag, 1986.

"Felipe 'El jipi.' " Comp. and perf. Lalo Guerrero. Rec. ca. 1965. Colonial, 589.

Fernández de Lizardi, José Joaquín ("El Pensador Mexicano"). *El periquillo sarniento.* Mexico City: Porrúa, 1976.

"Ferrocarrilero, El" (The railroad workman). Diálogo cómico. Perf. Consuelo Contreras and Eduardo Carrillo. Rec. Chicago, 19 June 1928. Victor, 81572.

"Fifís, Los." Broadside (UCLA Library, Special Collections). Testamentaria Vanegas Arroyo No. 21. Mexico City, January 1918.

Flores, Lauro. "La dualidad del pachuco." *Revista Chicano-Riqueña* 4.6 (1978): 51–58.

———. "Narrative Strategies in Rolando Hinojosa's *Rites and Witnesses.*" In Saldívar, *Hinojosa Reader* 170–179.

Foley, John Miles. *The Theory of Oral Composition: History and Methodology.* Bloomington: Indiana University Press, 1988.

Forster, E. M. *Aspects of the Novel.* 1927. New York: Harcourt Brace Jovanovich, 1955.

Fraire-Aldava, Eugene. "Octavio Romano's 'Goodby Revolution, Hello Slum': A Study of Ironic Tone and Meaning." *Aztlán: Chicano Journal of the Social Sciences and the Arts* 3.1 (1972): 165–69.

Frischmann, Donald H. "El Teatro Campesino y su mito *Bernabé:* Un regreso a la madre tierra." *Aztlán: International Journal of Chicano Studies Research* 2.12 (1981): 259–270.

Frye, Northrop. *Anatomy of Criticism.* Princeton: Princeton University Press, 1973.

Fuentes, Victor. "Luis Valdez: De Delano a Holliwood." *Rayas* 3.2 (1979): 10.

Galarza, Ernesto. *Barrio Boy.* Notre Dame: University of Notre Dame Press, 1971.

Galván, Roberto A., and Richard V. Teschner. *El diccionario del español chicano.* Silver Springs, Md.: Institute of Modern Languages, 1975.

Gamio, Manuel. *Mexican Immigration to the United States.* New York: Dover, 1971.

García, Nasario. "Satire: Techniques and Devices in Luis Valdez's 'Las dos caras del patroncito.' " *De Colores: Journal of Chicano Expression and Thought* 4.1 (1975): 66–74.

García Cubas, Antonio. *El libro de mis recuerdos.* 2d. ed. Mexico City: Imprenta Manuel León Sánchez, 1934.

Geertz, Clifford. *The Interpretation of Cultures: Selected Essays.* New York: Basic Books, 1973.

Gehman, Henry Snyder, ed. *Westminster Dictionary of the Bible.* Philadelphia: Westminster, 1970.

Gilman, Stephen. "The Death of Lazarillo de Tormes." *PMLA* 81.3 (1966): 149–166.

Gonzales, Juan. "Forgotten Pages: Spanish Language Newspapers in the Southwest." *Journalism History* 4.2 (1977): 50–51.

Gonzales, Juan L., Jr. *Mexican and Mexican American Farm Workers: The California Agricultural Industry.* New York: Praeger, 1985.

Gonzales-Berry, Erlinda. "Estampas del Valle: From Costumbrismo to Self-reflecting Literature." *Bilingual Review* 7.1 (1980): 29–38.

González Obregón, Luis. "Currutacas y petimetres." In *A ustedes les consta: Antología de la crónica en México,* ed. Carlos Monsiváis, 115–121. Mexico City: Ediciones Era, 1981.

Grajeda, Rafael. "Jose Antonio Villarreal and Richard Vasquez: The Novelist against Himself." In *The Identification and Analysis of Chicano Literature,* ed. Francisco Jiménez. Jamaica, N.Y.: Bilingual Press/Editorial Bilingüe, 1979.

Gramsci, Antonio. *Selections from Cultural Writings.* Edited by David Forgacs and Geoffrey Nowell-Smith. Trans. William Boelhower. Cambridge: Harvard University Press, 1985.

Griffin, Dustin. "Satiric Closure." *Genre* 18 (1985): 173–189.

Grismer, Raymond L. *The Influence of Plautus in Spain before Lope de Vega.* New York: Hispanic Institute in the United States, 1944.

Guilhamet, Leon. *Satire and the Transformation of Genre.* Philadelphia: University of Pennsylvania Press, 1987.

Guillén, Claudio. "La disposición temporal del *Lazarillo de Tormes.*" *Hispanic Review* 25 (1957): 264–279.

———. "Toward a Definition of the Picaresque." In *Literature as System: Essays toward the Theory of Literary History,* 71–106. Princeton: Princeton University Press, 1971.

Gumperz, John J., and Eduardo Hernández-Chávez. "Cognitive Aspects of Bilingual Communication." In *El Lenguage de los Chicanos: Regional and Social Characteristics Used by Mexican Americans,* ed. Eduardo Hernández-Chávez et al., 154–169. Arlington, Va. Center for Applied Linguistics, 1975.

Gutiérrez, Félix. "Spanish-Language Media in America: Background, Resources, History." *Journalism History* 4.2 (1977): 34+.

Gutiérrez, José Angel. *A Gringo Manual on How to Handle Mexicans.* Crystal City, Tex.: Wintergarden Publishing, n.d.

Guzmán, Ralph. "Mexican American Casualties in Vietnam." *La Raza* 1.1 (n.d.): 12–15.

Habermas, Jürgen. *Historia y crítica de la opinion pública: La Transformación estructural de la vida pública.* 2d. ed. trans. Antonio Deménech and Rafael Grasa. Mexico City: Gustavo Gili, 1981.

———. *The Philosophical Discourse of Modernity.* Trans. Frederic Lawrence. Cambridge: MIT Press, 1987.

Hernández, Guillermo E. *Canciones de la Raza: Songs of the Chicano Experience.* Berkeley: El Fuego de Aztlán, 1978.

———. "On the Theoretical Bases of Chicano Literature." *De Colores: Jour-

nal of Chicano Expression and Thought (Special Issue on Contemporary Chicano Literary Criticism) 5.1–2 (1980): 5–8.

———. "Interview with Rolando Hinojosa." Austin, 7 July 1985.

———. "Interview with José Montoya." Sacramento, 14 December 1986.

———. "Interview with Luis Valdez." Los Angeles, 19 December 1986.

———. "El México de fuera: Notas para su historia cultural." *Cuadernos Americanos* 259.2 (1985): 101–119.

Hernández-Chávez, Eduardo, Andrew Cohen, and Anthony F. Beltramo, eds. *El Lenguaje de los Chicanos: Regional and Social Characteristics Used by Mexican Americans.* Arlington, Va.: Center for Applied Linguistics, 1975.

Herrera-Sobek, María. *Beyond Stereotypes: The Critical Analysis of Chicana Literature.* Binghamton, N.Y.: Bilingual Press/Editorial Bilingüe, 1985.

Hinojosa-Smith, Rolando. *Claros varones de Belken: Fair Gentlemen of Belken County.* Tempe, Ariz.: Bilingual Press/Editorial Bilingüe, 1986.

———. "Crossing the Line: The Construction of a Poem." In Saldívar, *Hinojosa Reader* 25–38.

———. *Estampas de valle y otras obras.* Berkeley: Quinto Sol Publications, 1973.

———. *Generaciones y semblanzas.* Berkeley: Justa Publications, 1977.

———. *Klail City: A Novel.* Houston: Arte Público Press, 1987.

———. *Klail City y sus alrededores.* Havana: Casa de las Américas, 1976.

———. *Korean Love Songs: From Klail City Death Trip.* Berkeley: Justa Publications, 1978.

———. *Mi querido Rafa.* Houston: Arte Público Press, 1981.

———. *Partners in Crime: A Rafe Buenrostro Mystery.* Houston: Arte Público Press, 1985.

———. *Rites and Witnesses: A Comedy.* Houston: Arte Público Press, 1982.

———. "The Sense of Place." In Saldívar, *Hinojosa Reader* 18–24.

———. "A Voice of One's Own." In Saldívar, *Hinojosa Reader* 11–17.

———. "Writing Is Not a Process." Paper presented at the First Midwest Symposium on la Cultura Chicana: Twenty-five Years of the Chicano Novel. Madison, Wis., 23 November 1987.

Hirsch, E. D., Jr. *Validity in Interpretation.* New Haven: Yale University Press, 1967.

Hohendahl, Peter Uwe. "Critical Theory, Public Sphere, and Culture: Jürgen Habermas and His Critics." *New German Critique* 16 (1979): 89–118.

Huerta, Jorge A. "Chicano Teatro: A Background." *Aztlán: Chicano Journal of the Social Sciences and the Arts* 2.2 (1971): 63–78.

———. *Chicano Theater: Themes and Forms.* Ypsilanti, Mich.: Bilingual Press/Editorial Bilingüe, 1982.

Hunter, R. L. *The New Comedy of Greece and Rome.* Cambridge: Cambridge University Press, 1985.

"Inundación of [sic] California, La." Perf. (Elena) Ramírez Domínguez and

Fierro (Cancioneros Acosta). Comp. Eduardo Tavo and E. V. Escalante. Rec. San Francisco, 29 March 1928. Okeh, 16285.

Jacobson, Rodolfo. "The Social Implications of Intra-Sentencial Code-Switching." *New Scholar* 6 (1977): 227–256.

Jameson, Fredric. *The Political Unconscious*. Ithaca: Cornell University Press, 1981.

Jiménez, A. *Nueva picardía mexicana*. Mexico City: Editores Mexicanos, 1982.

Jiménez, Francisco. "Dramatic Principles of the Teatro Campesino." *The Identification and Analysis of Chicano Literature*. New York: Bilingual Press/Editorial Bilingüe, 1979.

Johnson, Samuel. *Dictionary of the English Language*. 1755. Reprint. Philadelphia: Jacob Johnson, 1805.

Jones, C. P. *Culture and Society in Lucian*. Cambridge: Harvard University Press, 1986.

Kanellos, Nicolas, ed. *Mexican American Theater: Then and Now*. Houston: Arte Público Press, 1983.

Kernan, Alvin B. *The Plot of Satire*. New Haven: Yale University Press, 1965.

Kirk, Eugene P. *Menippean Satire: An Annotated Catalogue of Texts and Criticism*. New York: Garland, 1980.

Konstan, David. *Roman Comedy*. Ithaca: Cornell University Press, 1983.

Luis Leal, ed. *Aztlán y México: Perfiles literarios e históricos*. Binghamton, N.Y.: Bilingual Press/Editorial Bilingüe, 1985.

———. "Chicano Journals (1970–1979)." In Leal, *Aztlán y México* 100–109.

———. "Female Archetypes in Mexican Literature." In *Women in Hispanic Literature*, ed. Beth Miller. Berkeley: University of California Press, 1983.

———. "History and Memory in *Estampas del valle*." In Saldívar, *Hinojosa Reader* 101–132.

———. "Mexican American Literature: A Historical Perspective." In *Chicano Writers: A Collection of Critical Essays*, ed. Joseph Sommers and Tomás Ybarra-Frausto, 18–30. Englewood Cliffs, N.J.: Prentice-Hall, 1979.

———. "Narrativa chicana: Viejas y nuevas tendencias." In Leal, *Aztlán y México* 111–120.

———. "Pícaros y léperos en la narrativa mexicana." In Leal, *Aztlán y México* 209–216.

Lesy, Michael. *Wisconsin Death Trip*. New York: Pantheon Books, 1973.

Limón, José E. "Agringado Joking in Texas Mexican Society: Folklore and Differential Identity." *New Scholar* 6 (1977): 33–50.

———. "The Folk Performance of 'Chicano' and the Cultural Limits of Political Ideology." In *"And Other Neighborly Names": Social Process and Cultural Image in Texas Folklore*, ed. Richard Bauman and Roger D. Abrahams. Austin: University of Texas Press, 1981.

Lint, Robert G. "Art in Montoya's 'Resonant Valley.'" *La Luz* 3.12 (1975): 40.

Lloyd, G. E. R. *Polarity and Analogy: Two Types of Argumentation in Early Greek Thought.* Cambridge: Cambridge University Press, 1966.

Lomelí, Francisco A., and Donaldo W. Urioste, eds. *Chicano Perspectives in Literature: A Critical and Annotated Bibliography.* Albuquerque: Pajarito Publications, 1976.

Lord, Albert B. *The Singer of Tales.* New York: Atheneum, 1971.

Loyal, C. [María Amparo de Burton]. *The Squatter and the Don: Descriptive of Contemporary Occurrances in California.* San Francisco: Samuel and Carson, 1885.

Lucian, "Philosophies for Sale (Vitarum Auctio)." Trans. A. M. Harmon. Edited by E. H. Warmington. Loeb Classical Library 2. Cambridge: Harvard University Press, 1968.

Macías, Ysidro Ramón. "The Evolution of the Mind." *El Pocho Che* 1.1 (1969): N.p.

McWilliams, Carey. *North from Mexico: The Spanish-Speaking People of the United States.* New York: Greenwood Press, 1968.

Madrid-Barela, Arturo. "In Search of the Authentic Pachuco: An Interpretive Essay." *Aztlán: Chicano Journal of the Social Sciences and the Arts* 1.4 (1973): 31–60.

———. "Pochos: The Different Mexicans, An Interpretive Essay, Part I." *Aztlán International Journal of Chicano Studies Research* 1.7 (1976): 51–64.

Magaña Esquivel, Antonio. *Medio siglo de teatro mexicano, 1900–1961.* Mexico City: Instituto Nacional de Bellas Artes, 1964.

"Magnífica es la campaña contra los 'fifís.'" *La Prensa* (San Antonio), 20 June 1923, 1.

María y Campos, Armando de. *El teatro del género chico en la revolucíon mexicana.* Mexico City: Instituto de Estudios Históricos de la Revolución Mexicana, 1956.

Mazón, Mauricio. *The Zoot-Suit Riots: The Psychology of Symbolic Annihilation.* Austin: University of Texas Press, 1984.

Meléndez, Theresa. "Coyote: Towards a Definition of a Concept." *Aztlán: International Journal of Chicano Studies Research* 13.1–2 (1982): 295–307.

Meyer, Doris L. "Early Mexican-American Responses to Negative Stereotyping." *New Mexico Historical Review* 53.1 (1978): 75–91.

Miller, Beth, ed. *Women in Hispanic Literature: Icons and Fallen Idols.* Berkeley: University of California Press, 1983.

Moers, Ellen. *The Dandy: Brummell to Beerbohm.* Lincoln: University of Nebraska Press, 1978.

Montoya, José. "Casindio: Chicano Music All Day." El Trio Casindio and the Royal Chicano Air Force. A Nonántzin Production. Elmira, Calif.: Instituto de Lengua y Cultura, 1985.

———. "In Formation: The Selected Poems of José Montoya/The RCAF: A Retrospect. San Jose, Calif.: Chusma House, in press.

———. "El Louie." In *Aztlán: An Anthology of Mexican American Literature,* ed. Luis Valdez and Stan Steiner. New York: Vintage Books, 1972.

———. "Marinero mariguano." Personal tape recording. Sacramento, 1985.

———. *El sol y los de abajo and Other RCFA Poems*. San Francisco: Ediciones Pocho-Che, 1972.

Morin, Raul. *Among the Valiant: Mexican-Americans in WWII and Korea*. Los Angeles: Borden Publishing, 1963.

Morton, Carlos. "Platicando con Luis Valdez." *Rayas: Newsletter of Chicano Arts and Literature* 4 (1978): 12+.

———. "La Serpiente Shreds Its Own: Changes in Aztlán." *La Luz* 8–9.4 (1975): 26–28.

"Norms in Satire: A Symposium." *Satire Newsletter* 2.1 (1964): 2–25.

Ong, Walter J. *Orality and Literacy: The Technologizing of the Word*. New York: Methuen, 1982.

Ortega y Medina, Juan A. *México en la conciencia anglosajona*. Vol. 1 México y lo Mexicano 13. Mexico City: Porrúa y Obregón, 1953.

———. *México en la conciencia anglosajona*. Vol. 2. México y lo Mexicano 22. Mexico City: Antigua Librería Robredo, 1955.

Ortego, Philip D. "The Chicano Renaissance." In *La Causa Chicana: The Movement for Justice*, ed. Margaret M. Mangold, 42–64 . New York: Family Service Association of America, 1971.

Padilla, Ray. "Apuntes para la documentación de la cultura chicana." *El Grito* 5.2 (1971–72): 3–79.

Paredes, Américo. "The Anglo-American in Mexican Folklore." In *New Voices in American Studies*, ed. Ray B. Browne and Donald M. Winkelman. Lafayette: Purdue University Press, 1966.

———. "El folklore de los grupos de origen mexicano en los Estados Unidos." *Folklore Americano* (Lima, Peru) 14.14 (1964): 146–163.

———. "Folk Medicine and the Intercultural Jest." In *Spanish-Speaking People in the United States*, ed. June Helm. Proceedings of the 1968 Annual Spring Meeting of the American Ethnological Society. Seattle: University of Washington Press, 1968.

———. "On Ethnographic Work among Minority Groups: A Folklorist's Perspective." *New Scholar* 6 (1977): 1–32.

———. *A Texas-Mexican "Cancionero": Folksongs of the Lower Border*. Urbana: University of Illinois Press, 1976.

———. *"With His Pistol in His Hand": A Border Ballad and Its Hero*. 1958. Austin: University of Texas Press, 1981.

Paredes, Raymund A. "Autobiography and Ethnic Politics." *a/b: Autobiographical Studies* (Fall 1987): 30–38.

———. "The Evolution of Chicano Literature." In *Three American Literatures*, ed. Houston A. Baker, Jr. New York: MLA, 1982.

———. "The Origins of Anti-Mexican Sentiment in the United States." *New Scholar* 6 (1977): 139–165.

———. "Politics and Ethnic Autobiography: Richard Rodriguez's *Hunger of Memory*." In *American Autobiographies*, ed. Robert Payne. Knoxville: University of Tennessee Press, forthcoming.

"Payasa, La." Diálogo cómico. Perf. Netty y Jesús Rodríguez. Rec. San Antonio, 16 September 1937. Bluebird, 3113B.

Payne, F. Anne. *Chaucer and Menippean Satire*. Madison: University of Wisconsin Press, 1981.

Paz, Octavio. *El laberinto de la soledad*. Mexico City: Cuadernos Americanos, 1950.

Peschel-Tentsch, Dietmar. "José Montoya." In *Partial Autobiographers: Interviews with Twenty Chicano Poets,* ed. Wolfgang Binder. Erlanger: Palm and Enke, 1985.

Petro, Peter. *Modern Satire: Four Studies*. Berlin: Mouton Publishers, 1982.

Pettit, Arthur G. *Images of the Mexican American in Fiction and Film*. College Station: Texas A&M University Press, 1980.

"Pelonas, Las." Dueto veracruzano. Rec. Richmond, Ind., 27 August 1928. Gennett, 40160.

Poplack, Shana. "Sometimes I'll Start a Sentence en English Y TERMINO EN ESPAÑOL: Towards a Typology of Code Switching." *Linguistics* 18 (1980): 581–618.

Prieto, Guillermo. "Contra Juan Nepomuceno Almonte." In *Omnibus de poesía mexicana,* ed. Gabriel Zaid, 171. Mexico City: Siglo XXI Editores, 1971.

Ragué Arias, Maria José. "Conversación con Ronnie Davies." *Primer Acto* 135 (August 1971): 54–57.

Ramage, Edwin S. *"Urbanitas": Ancient Sophistication and Refinement*. Norman: University of Oklahoma Press, 1973.

Rawson, Claude, ed. *English Satire and the Satiric Tradition*. Oxford: Basil Blackwell, 1984.

"Raymundo 'El pachuco.' " Perf. Los Conejos and Los Alegres de Terán. Rec. ca. 1950. Columbia, 4076C.

Reyes de la Maza, Luis. *Circo, maroma y teatro, 1810–1910*. Mexico City: UNAM, 1985.

Reyna, José R. *Raza Humor: Chicano Joke Tradition in Texas*. San Antonio: Penca Books, 1980.

Riggan, William. *Pícaros, Madmen, Naifs, and Clowns: The Unreliable First-Person Narrator*. Norman: University of Oklahoma Press, 1981.

Ríos, Herminio, and Lupe Castillo. "Toward a True Chicano Bibliography: Mexican American Newspapers, 1848–1942." *El Grito* 3.4 (1970): 17–24.

Ríos-Bustamante, Antonio, and Pedro Castillo. *An Illustrated History of Mexican Los Angeles, 1781–1985*. Los Angeles: Chicano Studies Research Center, UCLA, 1986.

Robinson, Cecil. *With the Ears of Strangers*. Tucson: University of Arizona Press, 1963.

Robles, J. Humberto. *Los desarraigados*. Mexico City: Instituto Nacional de Bellas Artes, 1962.

Rodriguez, Richard. *Hunger of Memory: The Education of Richard Rodriguez*. New York: Bantam Books, 1982.

Rojas, Arnold R. *The Vaquero*. Santa Barbara: McNally and Loftin, 1964.

Rojas, Guillermo. "Toward a Chicano/Raza Bibliography: Drama, Prose, Poetry." *El Grito* 2.7 (1973): 1–56.

Romano-V, Octavio I. "The Historical and Intellectual Presence of Mexican-Americans." *El Grito* 2.2 (1969): 32–46.

Romo, Ricardo. "The Urbanization of Southwestern Chicanos in the Early Twentieth Century." *New Scholar* 6 (1977): 183–207.

Rosaldo, Renato, Jr., *When Natives Talk Back: Chicano Anthropology since the Late Sixties,* ed. Ignacio M. García, 3–20. Renato Rosaldo Lecture Series Monograph 2. Series 1984–85. Tucson: Mexican American Studies and Research Center, 1986.

Rosenheim, Edward W., Jr. *Swift and the Satirist's Art.* Chicago: University of Chicago Press, 1963.

Ruiz, Juan. "Arcipreste de Hita." In *Libro de Buen Amor,* ed. Julio Cejador y Frauca. 2 vols. Madrid: Espasa-Calpe, 1967.

Saldívar, José David, ed. *The Rolando Hinojosa Reader: Essays Historical and Critical* (Special issue of *Revista Chicano-Riqueña* 12.3–4 [1984]. Houston: Arte Público Press, 1985.

Saldívar, Ramón. "*Korean Love Songs:* A Border Ballad and Its Heroes." In Saldívar, *Hinojosa Reader* 143–157.

———. "Ideologies of the Self: Chicano Autobiography." *Diacritics* 15.3 (1985): 25–34.

Salinas, Raúl. *Un Trip through the Mind Jail y Otras Excursions.* San Francisco: Editorial Pocho-Che, 1980.

Sánchez, George I. "Pachucos in the Making." *Common Ground* 4 (1943): 13–50.

Sánchez, José María. "A Trip to Texas in 1828." *Southwestern Historical Quarterly* 39.4 (1926): 249–288.

Sánchez, Rosaura. "Chicano Bilingualism." *New Scholar* 6 (1977): 209–225.

———. "From Heterogeneity to Contradiction: Hinojosa's Novel." In Saldívar, *Hinojosa Reader* 76–100.

———. "Postmodernism and Chicano Literature." *Aztlán: International Journal of Chicano Studies Research* 18.2 (1987): 1–14.

———. "Spanish Codes in the Southwest." In *Modern Chicano Writers: A Collection of Critical Essays,* ed. Joseph Sommers and Tomás Ybarra-Frausto, 41–53. Englewood Cliffs, N.J.: Prentice-Hall, 1979.

Sánchez-Boudy, José. *Diccionario de cubanismos más usuales.* Miami: Ediciones Universal, 1978.

Santamaría, Francisco J. *Diccionario de mexicanismos.* Mexico City: Porrúa, 1959.

Santillana, Marqués de [Don Iñigo López de Mendoza]. "Proemio al condestable Don Pedro de Portugal." In *Crestomatía del Español Medieval,* ed. Ramón Menéndez Pidal, 578–583. 2nd ed. Vol. 2. Madrid: Gredos, 1966.

Segal, Erich. *Roman Laughter: The Comedy of Plautus.* 2d ed. New York: Oxford University Press, 1971.

Servín, Manuel P. "The Post-World War II Mexican-American, 1925–1965: A Non-Achieving Minority." In *An Awakening Minority: The Mexican-Americans,* ed. Manuel P. Servín, 160–174. 2d ed. Beverly Hills: Glencoe Press, 1974.

Shank, Theodore. "A Return to Mayan and Aztec Roots." *Drama Review* 4.18 (December 1974): 56–70.

Smith, Paul. *Discerning the Subject.* Theory and History of Literature 55. Minneapolis: University of Minnesota Press, 1988.

Stallybrass, Peter, and Allon White. *The Politics and Poetics of Transgression.* Ithaca: Cornell University Press, 1986.

Stefano, Onofre di. *"La Prensa* of San Antonio and Its Literary Page, 1913 to 1915." Ph.D diss., University of California at Los Angeles, 1983.

Stewart, Susan. *Nonsense: Aspects of Intertextuality in Folklore and Literature.* Baltimore: John Hopkins University Press, 1989.

Suárez, Mario. "Kid Zopilote." *Arizona Quarterly* 3.2 (1947): 130–137.

Teschner, Richard V., et al., eds. *Spanish and English of the United States: A Critical, Annotated, Linguistic Bibliography.* Arlington, Va.: Center for Applied Linguistics, 1975.

Theophrastus. *The Characters of Theophrastus.* ed. and trans. J. M. Edmonds. Loeb Classical Library 225. Cambridge: Harvard University Press, 1953.

Thorpe, Peter. "Great Satire and the Fragmented Form." *Satire Newsletter* 4 (1965): 89–93.

"Tin Tan" (Germán Valdés), actor. *El mariachi desconocido.* Dir. Gilberto Martínez Solares. Mexico City, 1953.

Treviño, Fernando M. "Standardized Terminology for Hispanic Populations." *American Journal of Public Health* 77.1 (1987): 69–71.

Trujillo, Charlie. *Soldados: Chicanos in Viet Nam.* San José, Calif. Chusma House, 1990.

Ulica, Jorge [Julio G. Arce]. *Crónicas diabólicas.* Comp. Juan Rodríguez. San Diego: Maize Press, 1982.

Urbina, Luis G. *"Ecos Teatrales" de Luis G. Urbina.* Edited by Gerardo Sáenz. Mexico City: Instituto Nacional de Bellas Artes, 1963.

Uribe Hernández, Marcela. "El currutaco por alambique: Edición y estudio." B.A. thesis, Universidad Iberoamericana, Mexico City, 1974.

Valdés, Gina. *Comiendo lumbre.* Colorado Springs: Maize Press, 1986.

Valdez, Luis. *Actos.* San Juan Bautista, Calif.: Cucaracha Press, 1971.

———. "History of the Teatro Campesíno." *La Raza* 6.1 (1971): 17–19.

———. *Pensamiento Serpentino: A Chicano Approach to the Theater of Reality.* San Juan Bautista, Calif.: Cucaracha Press, 1973.

———. *The Shrunken Head of Pancho Villa.* In *Necessary Theater: Six Plays about the Chicano Experience,* ed. Jorge Huerta. Houston: Arte Publico Press, 1989.

———. "El Teatro Campesino." *Ramparts Magazine* 5.2 (July 1966): 40–43.

———. "Teatro di mutamento sociale." *Sipario* 292–293.25 (August–September 1970): 44–45.

Valdez, Luis, and Stan Steiner, eds. *Aztlán: An Anthology of Mexican American Literature.* New York: Vintage, 1972.

Van Rooy, C. A. *Studies in Classical Satire and Related Literary Theory.* Leiden: E. J. Brill, 1965.

Vasconcelos, José. *"La Tormenta": Segunda parte de "Ulises Criollo."* 6th ed. Mexico City: Ediciones Botas, 1937.

Venegas, Daniel. *Las aventuras de don Chipote o cuando los pericos mamen.* Mexico City: Secretaría de Educación Pública, 1984.

Vera, Ron. "Observations on the Chicano Relationship to Military Service in Los Angeles County." *Aztlán: Chicano Journal of the Social Sciences and the Arts* 1. (1970): 27–37.

Villagómez, Lenny. "Minutes of MASC-MECHA." University of California, Berkeley, 1968. np.

Villalogín, Carlos. "Chin Chun Chan." Tenorio en solfa y otras obras. Benson Latin American Collection, University of Texas at Austin. MxAm/Mss/oo4.

Villanueva, Tino. *Chicanos: Antología histórica y literaria.* Mexico City: Fondo de Cultura Económica, 1980.

Villarreal, José Antonio. *Pocho.* 1959. New York: Doubleday, 1970.

Vodánovic, Sergio. "El delantal blanco." In *Teatro Chileno Contemporaneo,* ed. Julio Durán-Cerda. Mexico City: Aguilar, 1970.

Walker, Roger M. "'Con miedo de la muerte la miel non es sabrosa': Love, Sin, and Death in the *'Libro de buen amor.'*" *"Libro de Buen Amor" Studies,* ed. G. B. Gybbon-Monypenny, 231–252. London: Tamesis, 1970.

Weber, David J. *Myth and the History of the Hispanic Southwest.* Albuquerque: University of New Mexico Press, 1987.

Weber, Harold. "'The Jester and the Orator': A Re-examination of the Comic and the Tragic Satirist." *Genre* 2.13 (1980): 171–185.

Welsford, Enid. *The Fool: His Social and Literary History.* New York: Farrar and Rinehart, 1935.

Wentworth, Harold, and Stuart Berg Flexner, comps. and eds. *Dictionary of American Slang.* 2d ed. New York: Crowell, 1975.

Wiedemann, Thomas. *Greek and Roman Slavery.* Baltimore: Johns Hopkíns Univesity Press, 1981.

Williams, Raymond. *Marxism and Literature.* Oxford: Oxford University Press, 1977.

Worcester, David. *The Art of Satire.* Cambridge: Harvard University Press, 1940.

Yarbro-Bejarano, Yvonne. "From *Acto* to *Mito:* A Critical Appraisal of the Teatro Campesino." In *Modern Chicano Writers: A Collection of Critical Essays,* ed. Joseph Sommers and Tomás Ybarra-Frausto. Englewood Cliffs, N.J.: Prentice-Hall, 1979.

Ybarra-Frausto, Tomás. "The Chicano Movement and the Emergence of Chicano Poetic Consciousness." *New Scholar* 6 (1977): 81–109.

Zamora, Bernice. *Restless Serpents.* Menlo Park, Calif.: Diseños Literarios, 1976.

Index